Walking with Legends

WALKING WITH LEGENDS

Barry Martyn's
NEW ORLEANS JAZZ ODYSSEY

Edited by
MICK BURNS

With a Foreword by
BRUCE BOYD RAEBURN

Louisiana State University Press
Baton Rouge

Published by Louisiana State University Press
Copyright © 2007 by Louisiana State University Press
All rights reserved
Manufactured in the United States of America

An LSU Press Paperback Original
First printing

Designer: Michelle A. Neustrom
Typeface: Fournier MT, Pointedly Mad
Printer and binder: Edwards Brothers, Inc.

Library of Congress Cataloging-in-Publication Data
Martyn, Barry, 1941–
  Walking with legends : Barry Martyn's New Orleans jazz odyssey / edited by Mick Burns ;
with a foreword by Bruce Boyd Raeburn.
    p. cm. — (An LSU Press paperback original)
  Includes bibliographical references (p.   ).
  ISBN 978-0-8071-3276-0 (pbk. : alk. paper) 1. Martyn, Barry, 1941– 2. Jazz musicians—
Louisiana—New Orleans—Biography. 3. Jazz—Louisiana—New Orleans—History and
criticism. 4. New Orleans (Louisiana)—History. I. Burns, Mick, 1942– II. Title.
  ML423.M35A3 2007
  781.65092—dc22
  [B]

2007001094

Published with support from the Louisiana Sea Grant College Program, a part of the National
Sea Grant College Program maintained by the National Oceanic and Atmospheric Administra-
tion of the U.S. Department of Commerce.

The paper in this book meets the guidelines for permanence and durability of the Committee
on Production Guidelines for Book Longevity of the Council on Library Resources. ♾

Contents

Illustrations

First Legends of Jazz public performance (Santa Monica, California, 1973)
New Orleans Society Orchestra (Los Angeles, 1973)
Legends of Jazz with band bus (Los Angeles, 1975)
The Legends of Jazz
Andrew Blakeney
Louis Nelson
Barry Martyn, Louis Nelson (Ohio, 1975)
Adolphus Morris
Joe "Brother Cornbread" Thomas
Cozy Cole, Floyd Levin, Barry Martyn (California, 1976)
Barney Bigard
Benny Carter
On *The Dinah Shore Show* (Los Angeles, 1976)
"1000 Years of Jazz" show (New York, 1979)
Clyde Bernhardt
Floyd Turnham
Society Brass Band (New Orleans, early 1990s)
The Young Men of New Orleans (Finland, 2002)
Barry Martyn

Foreword

Drummer, record producer, bandleader, jazz researcher, and cigar-chomping raconteur Barry Martyn is a New Orleans original who happens to have been born in England. This might seem implausible, but it makes perfect sense to members of the New Orleans traditional jazz community, who view themselves as an extended family based on merit as much as nativity. One earns a place through a combination of musical talent, good works, and attitude, fueled by a desire to "be in that number." Martyn found his way to New Orleans because he knew in his heart that he belonged there. In responding to the music of sage practitioners such as the clarinetist George Lewis, he arrived with a sense of purpose, determined not only to learn from his musical heroes but also to really get to know them.

Barry landed well and did what was required of him. He remains one of the busiest musicians on the New Orleans scene and can reflect upon more than half a century of musical activity. His role as a standard-bearer for the New Orleans jazz drumming tradition, honoring the legacies of the African American musicians who taught and inspired him, affirms our appreciation that New Orleans drummers are craftsmen. It's always about who can play for the band and make it sound good. Although this book is about a "life in jazz," one might say that the accent falls mainly on *life* because the narrative is primarily about the human relationships that make the music possible.

Martyn's homespun mode of expression and discourse is captivating, and the punch lines punctuating the exploits of the musicians who were his mentors enliven the telling of the tale tremendously. Barry has striven not to make this book too much about himself, and the care taken to recount the life stories of his associates renders the book especially meaningful. Intrinsic to the story is a continual clash of cultures—the avid pupil from the British Isles learning lessons of music (and life) from these elderly strangers, who take him under their wings partly out of self-interest and partly out of curiosity. Together, they find a way to connect through music, even if the road gets a little bumpy at times. This is a very moving story, full of anecdotal richness and maybe even a little didacticism (especially on racial injustice), pounding out ironies like drum strokes. It's an irresistible beat.

Mick Burns's masterful shaping of the text derives from decades of friendship with Barry Martyn, as well as an innate ability as a writer. It is a style that has been described as "gruff and crisp, without being over-articulate," a fitting complement to Martyn's modus operandi. Burns is also a musician in his own right, a trombonist, trumpeter, and tuba player with an abiding love for New Orleans music. He knows how to lace his annotations with a sly humor and what it takes to pace a narrative with judicious editing, as though he were constructing an extended solo on the bandstand. Quite frankly, he was the only man for the job. It's a collaboration that opens up a world few understood, let alone witnessed from the inside. You may not learn how to play drums in a jazz band by reading this book, but you'll definitely come away with an understanding of how New Orleans music can bring people of diverse backgrounds together.

Bruce Boyd Raeburn, Curator
Hogan Jazz Archive, Tulane University

Preface

I first met Barry Martyn in 1972. His regular trumpet player, Yoshio Toyama, was leaving his band to return to Japan, and the booking agent who worked for both of us sent me to try out for the job; I was playing trumpet at that time. This in itself was fairly unusual; agents do not usually have anything to do with bandleaders' hiring and firing, but I guess the guy was trying to do us both a favor.

The audition took place on one of Barry's jobs, at the Bedford Hotel, in Balham, South London. The Bedford was a huge place. It had been built in the earlier years of the century, one of hundreds of drinking palaces for the working classes erected in cities all over England. By 1972, it had fallen on hard times. It was just too damn big. Maintenance, heating, refurbishment, cleaning and adequate staffing costs were prohibitive, and the management bowed to economic pressure by cutting out most of these fripperies. As a result, the place had the surreal and desolate air of a lost city in the jungle. It also had an appropriate feeling of menace; Barry's clarinet player, John Defferay, had lost the seat of his trousers to the landlord's dog!

The Bedford's one reminder of its halcyon days was a big wooden circular stage, right in the middle of the place. This clanked, rumbled, shuddered, and revolved, clockwise, at about four miles per hour. From the band's perspective, this meant that the audience constantly disappeared to the left, while a new lot arrived from the right. It was a bit disconcerting, trying to establish any kind of rapport with a disappearing audience.

The Bedford was patronized by various groups of local residents. There was a bunch of elderly West Indian guys in zoot suits and porkpie hats, some red-faced Irish working men, a sprinkling of economy hookers, and a collection of human flotsam who looked as if they'd decided to postpone suicide until tomorrow. About ten o'clock, the West Indian guys would dance, on their own, cradling their beer, hats tipped forward, smiling, with their eyes closed.

The band opened with Yoshio on trumpet, and I sat and listened. I remember being fairly mystified by what the band was doing, particularly the eclectic repertoire. By the time it was my turn to play, I was more or less baffled—I just wasn't familiar with the band's idiom at that time. As I recall, the result was musically acceptable if unspectacular. Yoshio came back for the last set, Barry and I exchanged a courteous, if restrained, good night, and I left.

Around about 1988, I switched from playing trumpet to trombone. I thought, "To hell with him, he's not going to call now."

Which just shows how wrong you can be. The following year I met Barry again when I played trombone in his Eagle Brass Band in New Orleans, which I enjoyed very much, particularly playing alongside veteran trombonist Wendell Eugene.

In 1999, I was working on a book called *The Great Olympia Band*. Barry's help in completing the project was invaluable, and has remained so in supporting everything else I've done to date, including a second book—*Keeping the Beat on the Street*—and three radio documentaries.

This current book wasn't my idea originally. I was talking to my friend Peter Nissen, the Danish drummer and author, when he said, "Tell Barry he should write his memoirs; there would be so much to say." I duly passed this on, but Barry said, "I haven't got time to do that. Mind you, I'd be very happy if *you* were to do it." I knew he'd already turned two or three potential biographers down, so I was slightly flattered.

Anyway, we talked about it a bit, and both of us agreed that the main value of such a book would be recording his experience with the old-time musicians of New Orleans, all of whom have now passed on; there's relatively little emphasis on his English career.

For the whole of November 2004 we sat out on the deck of his house on Burgundy Street, fortified by coffee, cigars, and other smoking materials, generally starting at 6:30 a.m., with a tape recorder between us. Barry's natural skill as a raconteur, coupled with his phenomenal memory, took over, and by the end of the month, we'd amassed over forty hours of audiotape.

The results were as we had both intended. The story gives unique personal glimpses of a vanished generation of New Orleans musicians, including Barney Bigard, Zutty Singleton, Louis Armstrong, Billie and De De Pierce, John Handy, Andrew Morgan, Sammy Penn, George Lewis, Jim Robinson, Kid Howard, Alex Bigard, Ed Garland, Alton Purnell, Kid Sheik Cola, Emile Barnes, Joe Darensbourg, George Guesnon, Harold Dejan, Cié Frazier, Louis Nelson, Joe Watkins, Albert Nicholas, Peter Bocage, Brother Cornbread Thomas, Kid Thomas, Percy Humphrey, and Andrew Blakeney. From outside New Orleans there are some other legends—Ray Nance, Ben Webster, Joe Venuti, Benny Carter, and Hoagy Carmichael—and brief appearances by Nijinsky, Jayne Mansfield, Johnny Carson, Christine Keeler, Dinah Shore, and John Wayne.

Where else could you meet all these people?

Mick Burns

1941–1960
ENGLAND AND CANADA

In the decade following World War II, England was a bleak place, bedevilled by shortages of almost everything, stultified by a rigid class system, still dreaming of a rapidly disintegrating empire and exhausted by six years of a war that had left the country victorious but on the ropes. And it rained a lot. Mind you, we made our own amusement, which, in true English fashion, wasn't much fun. Take popular music. The radio played an insipid diet of crooners bleating about unrequited love (although not, of course, passion—this was England), novelty orchestras full of accordions (or worse still, banjos), and most depressing of all, cheerful novelty numbers about Little Red Monkeys or the imminent arrival of fishing fleets.

Or there was live music. Three or four nights a week, the mating rituals of the working class were conducted in thousands of dance halls throughout the country. The town I lived in had 60,000 inhabitants and five self-styled "ballrooms," all of which employed live bands of between five and twelve musicians. These guys were paid seven shillings and sixpence (75 cents) to regurgitate stock arrangements, which they did with all the enthusiasm and involvement of a typing pool. The music echoed the spirit of the country—uninspired and dull.

Small wonder that so many thousands of English men and women emigrated to former colonies Canada and Australia, which offered higher standards of living, relative freedom from class distinction and the chance of a fresh start. It would be gratuitously offensive to say anything about rats and sinking ships.

For young people growing up at that time, the years between childhood and adulthood were a strange kind of limbo. Young people were pretty much left to get on with it, which is precisely what they did, inventing their own youth culture in the process. Sartorial mainstay was the duffel coat—on any given Saturday afternoon, the average English town center looked like the embarkation point for a North Sea convoy. Venue of choice was one of the growing number of coffee bars, and the hip drink was cappuccino.

For thousands of these youngsters, preferred listening was the sound of New Orleans jazz on records. It was an honest preference—these records weren't advertised widely or given extensive airplay. In retrospect, it's difficult to see why so many kids all over the country wound up listening to Louis Armstrong, Sidney Bechet, George Lewis, and Bunk Johnson. It's probably got something to do with the emotional impact and joyousness of the music, both qualities which were notably missing from an average English existence. The sounds that came out of the record player sounded to us like the voice of God, compared to the banality of the homegrown product.

We had all a romantic idea of New Orleans in our heads (and hearts) but this was as remote from the real place as Tennyson's Camelot, or the image broadcast by the city's tourist authority. Over the course of time, some people acquired musical instruments and tried to copy the sounds they had heard on the records. Bands emerged in which enthusiasm outweighed expertise in a ratio of about ten to one. Over the course of a few years, the musical standards and popularity of these British bands improved and attracted the attention of agents, promoters, record companies, and the media, including radio and television.

The original New Orleans model was dumbed down harmonically and rhythmically to an almost nursery-rhyme level. All the bands sounded pretty much the same and tried to create an identity by using silly stage clothes— Confederate soldiers or eighteenth-century costume—and outlandish material ("Teddy Bears' Picnic" or Prokofiev's "Peter and the Wolf"). This music became known as "trad"—shorthand for "traditional jazz." The showbiz era that surrounded it, in which some people made a lot of money, was called the "trad boom."

Meanwhile, on the other side of the Atlantic, the real city of New Orleans had its own social and musical preoccupations.

I was born in England on February 23, 1941, with the name Barry Martyn Godfrey—but who the hell would remember a musician called Barry Godfrey? The first thing I remember is sitting in the garden, in Egham, Surrey. I was just a baby, and I remember we had two dogs, Punch and Pedro. This was during World War II—I must have been about three.

After the war when my daddy came back, my Aunt Doris would take me to Fortnum and Mason's to hear the tea orchestra. She'd take me there and buy me boxes of chocolates and we'd bring them home.

My daddy had set up as a plumber when he left the air force in 1945, but my aunt Elizabeth persuaded him to go into market gardening—she said that her husband Charlie was an expert. So they bought a piece of land together. They raised lettuces and stuff and took them to market at four o'clock in the morning. I remember my daddy saying that Charlie went there the first morning but after that he was too tired to go anymore. It was a one-sided partnership—daddy did all the work.

Near where we lived was the Holloway Sanatorium; it was a mental institution. All through the war, my uncle Charlie had worked there. He would steal the patients' food parcels, and during the worst of food rationing, my family would get delicacies like pickled walnuts and Stilton cheese.

Charlie died when I was quite young, and Aunt Elizabeth and my daddy kept the business going between them. Every day he would go delivering the produce with a big American Dodge V-8 truck. He put me in charge of boiling the beetroot. I had to go over there early. Sometimes I'd go to the market at Brentford with him at 4:00 a.m. I used to enjoy that, meeting all the porters and produce sellers. I was just a little boy, and they were all very kind to me; some of them would give me a bit of money to buy candy. Some of the people there wore suits, and some of them, the porters, were raggedy ass—they were the ones that pushed the barrows. In later years, when I was a musician, my daddy got me a porter's license, which meant that you could use this special pub that they had. All the other places would close around 11:00 p.m. but this place would open up at midnight and stay open until the early morning.

Anyway, back to boiling beetroot. They had a massive iron pot; you had to light a fire under it. I had to pull the beets from the field, take the tops off them, and throw them in the boiling water—it was freezing work and the beets really stank. To this day I have never eaten beetroot. I can't stand to look at them.

I used to go sometimes with my daddy on his delivery rounds and carry the stuff into the customers' houses. That's how I came to meet Nijinsky, the ballet dancer. To this day, people think I'm making it up. The delivery round included a big hotel called Great Fosters, and often there would be movie stars staying there. I remember seeing Ginger Rogers there, and Alan Ladd. But Nijinsky didn't stay there, he had his own house; I must have met him about twenty times. He could speak broken English; he was a nice old man. Round about 1957, I met Bryan Forbes, the movie director, who opened a bookstore near where we lived. He was a well-known actor in England, but I don't think he'd started directing at that time. He and his wife, Nannette Newman, bought a house near there, and they were delivery customers of ours. I met Richard Attenborough through them, and they introduced me to Terry Thomas. Diana Dors had a home up there—she was a big movie star at that time. She was married to a guy named Dickie Dawson. In later years, when I was in California, I was watching *Hogan's Heroes* on TV, and there he was! When the credits came up, I saw that he was using the name Richard Dawson. He wound up being the host of a show called *Family Feud* in the U.S.—it was very popular.

My daddy was in a minstrel troupe; they called themselves the Virginia Minstrels. They would black up, and Daddy wore a big top hat—he was Mr. Interlocutor—that's like a master of ceremonies. Their big number was "McNamara's Band." They would rehearse in the front room at our house, so there were always instruments there. They couldn't play them, but they needed them for the "McNamara's Band" routine. There were trumpets, trombones, all that stuff. I would try to play them, and catch hell from my dad. Finally, when I was about twelve years old, I started banging on an old drum that was there, and I took a liking to it.

Round about then, I got in with a gang of bad boys. There was me, "Cousin" Jesse, Johnny Bray, "Bugs" Beaumont. We all wore black v-neck sweaters with a white stripe—we really thought we were something! It was a poor area we lived in, and if I hadn't left there, I'd probably have wound up in jail. Johnny Bray was going with Christine Keeler. Christine Keeler was to make it in an unorthodox way. In later years, her affair with Minister John Profumo was to cause the downfall of the Macmillan government. When I knew her, she was about twelve years old. She was old for her years, but not very good looking. She lived in a trailer park by Laleham with her mother. The headmaster told both of us we'd never amount to anything. I think we were the only two from that school that did.

At the same sort of time, I discovered a book called *Jazz* written by an English nitwit called Rex Harris. I guess he must be long gone. I was reading it in school one day, during a math class, and I caught hell from the teacher. After class, two boys came up and said, "We're jazz musicians." Their names were Peter Stempt and Geoffrey Beere. We decided to form a band together. Peter played alto sax, Geoffrey played trumpet, and I played drums. There were just the three of us, and we would play in an old air-raid shelter left over from the war. By then, I had saved up from various little jobs I had, delivering groceries and throwing papers, so I had bought a new snare drum—it cost nine pounds.

I still had the bass drum from the minstrel show. I painted a picture of the devil on it, and the name "Red Devils Jazz Band." We only knew one tune, "Weary Blues." If we played it slow, we called it "I'm Travelin'." Then we played it fast and called it "Shake It and Break It." They're all the same number. Sometimes friends would hire us to play at parties. At least they were friends when they hired us; by the time they turned us loose, I'm not so sure.

We used to get together when we were young; kids would bring their records to play. Things like Johnny Ray singing "Cry," Alma Cogan doing "Hernando's Hideaway," and other stuff like Ruby Murray or Lita Rosa. You went down big with the girls if you brought records to these things; it made you look hip. So I went to Maxwell's Music Store in my home town, but I didn't have a clue what to ask for. The sales clerk produced "Basin Street Blues" by Louis Armstrong's All Stars, so I bought that. The other kids laughed at it and threw me out. I didn't care; I went home and played it over and over. I preferred the music to the girls.

I went back to Maxwell's about a month later and asked the man, "Have you got any more of those records?" He said, "Yes, we've just had a delivery." They had some old coot singing "Land of Hope and Glory" and the George Lewis[1] band playing "Fidgety Feet" and "Dauphine Street Blues" on the Vogue label. So that was the second record I bought, and the die was cast. There was no going back. I didn't know the musicians were American, I didn't know they were black, but the beat and the joyousness of the music just took me.

Maxwell's gave me the catalog for Vogue records. I remember it listed something by Kid Ory's Creole Jazz Band—I thought the man's name was Kid Orys Creole. Just shows you how damn dumb I was.

I bought "Bobby Shaftoe" by Chris Barber. I could tell it was different music, but I couldn't have told you why. It was certainly easier to play the drums to; it was simple, just "thud, thud, thud."

The other guys in the Red Devils band told me that most of the records I was buying were by American musicians. The George Lewis record had "George Lewis and His New Orleans Stompers" on the label. That's the first time I heard of New Orleans; I certainly couldn't have found it on a map.

It was before rock 'n' roll, and it was a strange time for young people. There wasn't much to do. We used to go stealing lead off building sites to make a bit of money. One of us would keep watch on the roof of a new house, and the others would strip the lead off the roof. We'd take it back to the old air-raid shelter. We'd upturn some building bricks (which we'd also stolen). We'd melt the lead in a cauldron (my beet boiling experience came in useful) and tip it into the depressions in the bricks. It would set like bullion bars. We'd take the lead to a dealer a few miles away so it couldn't be traced. We were doing quite well until the day the lookout man on the roof fell asleep and didn't warn us the police were coming.

I jumped off into what I thought was just a pile of sand, but I was wrong: there was a cement mixer underneath. I broke my ankle, and all I could do was lay there and holler. The cop took me away to the police station. My mother came down there to plead with them. They let me go, but after that, I was scared to get up on those buildings any more.

When I was about thirteen, my family moved to Virginia Water. My daddy took a lease on a place over there. The only friend I had near the new place was called "Spud" Caldicott. He always wore a brown duffel coat, played a bit of guitar. He had a friend who played bass, named "Boxer" Bartlet, and we formed a sort of band together. The bass player had a friend who was a modern jazz guitarist, called Goudie Charles.

This dude was like something out of Minton's Playhouse. He had weird African shirts, a beret, and dark glasses. He was a real good musician. I gravitated to him—I didn't care what style it was. We got together with an alto player called Pete Buss and started a little bebop band.

Even today, all my technique with brushes comes from playing in that little band with Goudie Charles, rehearsing at my house. I don't think we ever got any jobs; we were a bit too modern for most people. So after about a year, we disbanded.

Then a couple of friends took me to Eel Pie Island. That was a place in the middle of the River Thames at Twickenham; you had to get there by boat. It was a hell of a place for young people that liked jazz, because you had all of the popular English bands. I must have been around sixteen at that time. It was a great big dance hall with a bar down one side and a bandstand at one end. Like a New Orleans dance hall, but bigger.

I met a guy there called Ken Palmer, who told me that his brother was a bouncer at Cy Laurie's club. I didn't know what a bouncer was, but I'd certainly heard of Cy Laurie: he was a well-known clarinet-playing English band leader. Ken Palmer's brother would sneak us into Cy's club up in London, and it was there that I met Gerry Green, a clarinet player who led a band called the Tivoli Gardens Orchestra; Gerry asked me to join the band. I remember the trumpet player was Clive Blackmore.

Clive had the best ear of anyone I've ever worked with. We could go to a record shop, play him a record of, say, Thomas Jefferson playing "Sugar Blues," and he'd play it on the job that night, after hearing it once. It was a four-piece band to start with: me, Gerry, Clive, and a banjo player called Ernest Larner. I had a letter from Ernest in 2001; he was a real nice guy.

We had to suspend the band for a while after one particular job, on a riverboat. The boat hit something below the waterline and keeled over, and the band all fell over the side into the river, including my drum kit! I never did get those drums back.

Shortly after that, I met a drummer called Alan Day. His father was a coal merchant and had made quite bit of money. When Alan was eighteen, his father asked him what he wanted for his birthday. Alan asked for this wooden coal shed they had next to the house. They opened it up as a jazz club. One of the band wives sat on the door and took the money, and musicians came there from all over. All of them tried to copy Bunk Johnson and the George Lewis band; they even called it San Jacinto Hall. It was the place to be on a Saturday night.

The English trombonist Mike Casimir had been to New Orleans and had actually met some of our heroes. He would come there and tell us about what color shirts Jim Robinson[2] wore and stuff like that. We'd sit around this big pot-bellied stove after the sessions finished and talk about Bunk and George Lewis until 4:00 a.m. God knows what we found to say, because we didn't know them, and none of us apart from Mike Casimir had been to New Orleans. This would be around 1957.

I was still with Gerry Green's little band, but we changed the name to the New Iberia Jazz Band, after Bunk's birthplace. Mike Casimir used to hire us to play with him, and somehow or other he took over the New Iberia name.

Keith Smith, the trumpet player, used to come and see us. He had his own band, but he was more interested in Ken Colyer.

I wasn't too much interested in Ken Colyer myself, and I'll tell you why. I remember one time, when I was maybe fifteen, I saw an advertisement in the *Sunday Express* newspaper advertising "Ken Colyer Jazzmen and for this one concert only the Omega New Orleans Brass Band." I said to my mother, "Look, there's a brass band from New Orleans playing in London tonight; I'd love to see that—can we go?"

We went up to the Stoll Theater, Kingsway, and sat through Ken Colyer's Jazzmen. I'd never heard of them. They were not too bad. Nothing like my records, but I was waiting to see the New Orleans Brass Band. When act two came, it was just the same guys with an added bass horn, second trumpet, and added saxes (Mole Benn bass horn, Neil Millet alto, Ken Saunders tenor, Sonny Morris trumpet). I never was so disappointed and vowed throughout my career I'd never refer to any band I had as a "New Orleans Band." You're deceiving the people, so I called anything I did from then on "New Orleans *style* band" or ". . . *style* drum playing." This Omega experience, the whole concert, was an Anglified version of what I was later to hear in New Orleans, almost a forerunner of English trad. Good for its time and place but the real McCoy, *no!*

Early in 1958, Keith Smith asked me to join his band. It was called the Fronz-I-Me band, after one of Bunk's bands. We opened a club in the Scout Hall in Tamworth, right in the middle of a field, and it was very popular. Keith wasn't a natural musician, but he worked hard at it, and I liked his playing. He was a go-ahead kind of guy. We used to travel to jobs in a little Austin Seven car. I was still working in the vegetable business during the day.

When George Lewis came to England in 1959, Keith and I wanted to find out when he was arriving so we could go and meet him. Keith said, "I know how to find out when George is coming. We'll go round and ask Ken Colyer." So we went round to Colyer's house, and he answered the door. He told us the wrong day—I don't know why—and Keith and I hung around Euston station for about three hours for nothing.

We went the next day and met George and the band. When the band arrived, it was like the arrival of Bill Haley and the Comets, except all the crowd were young kids with beards and duffel coats, long sweaters, all that. The girls—well, girls are always girls, you know what I mean. Somebody offered to carry Slow Drag's [Alcide Pavageau's] bass, and he wouldn't let them. All the trombone players, Johnny Mortimer, Pete Dyer, John Beecham, latched onto Jim Robinson. Pete was the most persistent, and he said, "Mr. Robinson, can I give you a lift to the hotel?" Pete had this tiny Messerschmitt bubble car. He opened the door, and Jim got in; when Pete went round the other side, Jim said, "What? You're getting in too?"

The band were staying at the Hotel Imperial, Russell Square, and we all used to hang around the lobby, just to catch a glimpse of them. I guess we were all fanatics.

George Lewis played the music I instinctively related to the most. It's like, when I was small, I would hear grown-up people talk about Enrico Caruso. One day, I was on the beach with my parents, and some people had a wind-up gramophone. There was this beautiful singing coming out, and I knew it was Caruso. Something inside my heart just told me. I was about eleven years old. It was the same kind of spiritual recognition with George Lewis. I just knew it was the real McCoy. It wasn't just that the musicians were American, it was more that black musicians played in a different way.

When you're at grade school in America, they give you an instrument and teach you to read music. In England, you would sing songs, and the music teacher would play you classical music and tell you how wonderful it was. Once a year, you could bring in records of the music you liked, and he'd explain how awful they were. So you can't expect people to come from that kind of background knowing anything about playing music.

In those days, the salesmen in record shops used to suggest things you might like, and that's how I came to buy a ten-inch pressing labeled "Bunk's Brass Band." I remember getting it home, and the first track I played was the slow hymn "Nearer My God to Thee." I couldn't believe it. I thought it was playing at the wrong speed. I tried playing it at 45 rpm instead of 33, and of course it sounded ridiculous. It was the first time I'd heard a funeral march beat. The bass drum player on that record is Lawrence Marrero. People say that Marrero was just a banjo player who played bass drum, but they don't realize that his drum teacher was Clay Jiles, one of the best bass drummers ever. But the more I listened, the more I liked it. I remember thinking that the clarinet playing sounded like somebody crying. I began to figure out that there was such a difference with that music. I didn't know what it was, but I wanted to find out.

From looking at photographs and movies, I started to put together a picture of New Orleans in my head. There was a guy called Rudy Marsalis—he was a black guy from New Orleans. With all us young musicians in London, he was like the oracle. We would buy him meals and drinks; he probably lived off us kids. But whatever he said, we believed, because we were interested in absorbing that culture. He was actually a bullshit artist of the first order. Whoever we asked him about—Bunk Johnson, Shots Madison—he claimed to know all of them. If we'd asked him, "Who do you know?" he wouldn't have been able to come up with one name.

By 1959, I had my own band, the Kid Martyn Ragtime Band, with some pretty classy musicians—Graham Paterson, Sammy Rimington, Pete Dyer, all them. But I still wanted to go to New Orleans, to see for myself, and see what I could learn. I knew I wasn't going to learn about it in England—you might as well try to learn to play cricket in New Orleans.

I had a friend called Anthony Parkhouse who had gone to live in Canada; he was what we called a commercial artist. He wrote to me from Montreal, all about what a wonderful country it was and how I should come out there. One day, I was walking by myself down the Haymarket in London, and I looked in the window of a travel shop. There was a poster saying "Come to New Orleans" and a photograph of Kid Sheik,[3] Percy Humphrey,[4] and Peter Bocage,[5] all dressed in brass band caps. I went right into the travel agent's and booked a passage on a boat. I left in May 1960 and went to Montreal. In those days, the Canadian government would sell you a one-way ticket for ten pounds, providing you stayed there for five years.

I came out of the office feeling good; I knew I was on my way. I went back home and told my girlfriend at that time, Carole, that I was going. She said to me, "I knew you would have to go sometime. I'll wait for you. If you don't go, you'll always regret it."

About a week after I got the ticket, I caught the train up to Liverpool. They allotted me a cabin on HMS *Carinthia*. The purser put me in with a Reverend Gray. I persuaded him I was unsuitable traveling company for a man of the cloth, and he switched me to a cabin with three other guys. They turned out to be serious drinkers. It was a good trip, took eight days; it was the best food I'd ever eaten, and we had lots of fun.

The boat docked at Montreal. Anthony Parkhouse met me and took me back to his apartment at 1425 St. Marc Street. Staying in Canada was a bit like a jail sentence, because I knew I was on my way to New Orleans, but it was a nice jail to be in. Montreal was a divided city, English and French (or rather, French Canadian—they don't like to be called French).

We went down to the local jazz club at a place called Moose Hall. I sat with the band, and they asked me to join, just like that! I thought that maybe I could make a living playing with them, but they only had one job a week. All the band were English except the banjo player. We later went on to win a radio competition. The clarinet player, Bob Wright, was the only one interested in New Orleans, and we later formed a quartet to play that style of music and to get more income.

While I was playing at Moose Hall in Montreal, all kinds of people would drop by. A piano player sat in with us, and he was really great. During the intermission he said, "I love your drumming. It's really pure African. Do you mind if I sit in again and record it?" I later found out that I'd recorded with Duke Jordan, who'd written "Jordu," recorded with Clifford Brown, all that.

I still had to find a day job. They were advertising for people to break rocks on the Trans-Canada Highway. I wasn't trained to do anything in particular, and I was young, strong, and foolish, so I decided to give it a try. I collapsed in the heat after about two hours and decided it wasn't for me.

Then I saw in the want ads a vacancy for something called a "shoe filer." I caught the bus out to an industrial park, to a place called Gladstone's Shoes. They said, "What experience have you had?" I told them, "None. I'm a musician." They asked me, "Are you interested in hard work?" I said, "Very interested." Which I was. So they gave me the job. It was a family business—the daddy and two sons, Norman and Sidney; a floorwalker, Ronnie Embree; and a guy called Marcel Duchamp, who was mainly interested in when the doughnut truck would be coming.

I lived, very frugally, off my musical earnings, and deposited my wage check in the bank every Friday. I had a black corduroy jacket, black pants, one white shirt and one black shirt—that was all the clothes I had.

At Gladstone's Shoes they had a Hungarian guy called Joe Horvath, looked just like Tin Tin out of the comic books. He was the biggest bullshitter I've ever met. He told me he was a prizefighter. He told me they had prizefights up in Quebec, and if I put my money on him, he'd knock everybody down. Like a fool, I went up there and I put a hundred dollars on him. He told me, "We turn that into five hundred dollars, just like that." It turned out he was a canvas freak. The first punch and he was out for the count, and I lost a hundred dollars. From that day to this, I've never gambled. If I go to Las Vegas, I don't put one nickel in those machines.

Anyway, it got to be New Year's Eve 1960. By then, I'd amassed about three thousand dollars. We played at a fraternity house that evening, and after the job, Bob Wright carried me to the Greyhound bus depot. He was crying; we'd been close. I remember saying to him, "Bob, maybe our paths will cross again." They did, but not until thirty-seven years later, in New Orleans.

1961–1972
NEW ORLEANS AND ENGLAND

Outside New Orleans, people who had never been there (especially jazz fans) had their own romantic image of the place, which included the scent of magnolias, moonlight on the Mississippi, and a nostalgic view of music they had picked up from listening to records. The real city had many thriving traditions, but Dixieland music (the description used by most of the musicians who played it) wasn't amongst them; New Orleans was more focused on political corruption on a breathtaking scale, criminality, violence, and institutionalized racism.

It was the racism that filtered through into the music; the black origins of the art made it intrinsically worthless in the eyes of the white population (although many of the white-only clubs insisted on hiring black orchestras for dancing; the beat was better). Under the hysterical headline "Unspeakable Jazz Must Go!" the city's Times-Picayune newspaper denied that New Orleans had anything to do with the birth of jazz.

When the English jazz critic James Asman visited New Orleans in the early 1960s, he appeared on a local radio show and was invited to choose some records. Not only did the station not have copies of his chosen records, they didn't have any music by any black bands at all.

For most of the black population (except the real old-timers) things had simply moved on—they were listening to big bands and, later, rhythm and blues. The older style of playing was regarded as "Uncle Tom." There wasn't much work for the great originals, many of whom were still alive in the early sixties.

Interest in the old-style music came mainly from out-of-towners, the most influential of whom was Bill Russell. Russell was no amateur enthusiast; he had a degree in music and a "serious" musical background. As a composer, his work had been recognized by, among others, John Cage; as a percussionist, he had worked for several years with a Chinese puppet theater; and although no violin virtuoso, he was at least proficient enough to give lessons.

Because he loved the music so much and understood its artistic importance, in 1942 he came to New Orleans and began to record generally unknown black musicians for posterity. He himself said, "It was simply the best music I ever heard, and so I recorded it." For three years between 1942 and 1945, he single-

handedly carried the crippling weight of a recording machine and glass-based acetates to small dance halls and musicians' houses, paying the musicians' wages out of his own pocket. Sales of the resulting records were derisory, but the music's beauty and power was to have an influence that was both international and lasting.

Russell's American Music label was a beacon to New Orleans music for others. Over the next twenty-five years enthusiasts inspired by Russell's example and similarly disdainful of commercial considerations recorded dozens of musicians, many of whom were playing as well as they ever did.

Although generally called the New Orleans Revival, it's more accurate to regard this music as a final flowering. When this musical generation was gone, its music was gone, too. But thanks to Heywood Broun, Sam Charters, Herbert Otto, Grayson Mills, Alden Ashforth, David Wyckoff, Joe Mares, Rudi Blesh, Barry Martyn, and—mainly—Bill Russell, recordings of this beautiful music survive.

⚓ 1961

I got on the bus and slept until I had to get off at Rouse's Point, the Canuck side of Burlington, Vermont. I wasn't supposed to leave Canada, and I didn't know if they'd let me in to the United States; I had no visible means of support. I got off the bus, drank a cup of coffee at the bus depot, turned right, and walked for about two miles. I saw this man digging a hole and asked him, "Is this the United States?" He said, "What are you, some kind of nut? Of course it's the United States!"

I hitched a ride into Burlington and caught a bus to New York City. I checked into the YMCA by Penn Station. After I'd slept for a bit, I got hold of a phone directory and looked up Arthur Singleton.[6] The address was the Alvin Hotel, right across from Birdland, 52nd and Broadway. I called the number and a man answered. I said, "Is this Mr. Arthur Singleton?" He said, "Yeah, but everybody calls me Zutty. Who is this?" I told him my name and that I was a drummer from England. He said, "You here in New York? Come on over." I said, "Wait a minute. You must be mistaking me for somebody else. I don't actually know you." He said, "Well, how am I going to know you if you don't come on over?"

I couldn't believe it. To make a comparison, you couldn't approach most English bandleaders at that time, and here's a jazz legend, Zutty Singleton, acting like he knows me. I knocked on his door, and he answered. As we walked down the hallway, he said, "Are you into jazz drumming?" and he showed me a picture of himself with Louis Armstrong's Savoy Ballroom Five. I named all the people in the picture, and he said, "How do you know that? You been here before?"

He introduced me to his wife, Marge, who was the sister of Charlie Creath, the St. Louis trumpet player. It was like I'd known her for twenty years, and we carried on talking until ten o'clock at night. He pointed out Birdland, right across the street. "All my friends play there," he told me. "Dizzy, Bird, Bud Powell. . . ." I realized that he didn't draw any distinctions between musical styles—it was all just music to him. He told me he was playing at Jimmy Ryan's on Wednesday, and I went to see him there.

There was a whole wall painted with the sign "Jimmy Ryan's, Home of Dixieland Jazz. Resident Band, Wilbur De Paris. Intermission Don Frye." On the Wednesdays and weekends, Tony Parenti and Zutty played the intermission with Don Frye. Zutty was one of the friendliest men I'd ever met.

To back up a little bit, when I lived in England, we had run benefit concerts and raised money for various New Orleans musicians who were sick and couldn't work, including Punch Miller. It was through these contacts that I had started corresponding with Alex Bigard,[7] the drummer (everybody called him Alec). Louis Armstrong's All Stars had done a concert in Montreal when I was living there, and I went backstage after the show. I introduced myself to Trummy Young and told him I was on my way to New Orleans. I said, "I'd really like to meet Barney Bigard,[8] because he's from there." Trummy said, "Go and tell him hello. He's sitting over there." Barney was sitting messing around with his clarinet reed, and I walked over and said, "Mr. Bigard, I'm a drummer from England. I correspond with your brother in New Orleans." He gave me a glacial stare and said "So?" I thought he was the opposite of Zutty; I later found differently.

Anyway, I stayed in New York about a week and heard Red Allen and Gene Krupa at the Metropole. Then I got the Greyhound bus to New Orleans, on a one-way ticket. It took forty-one hours to get there. When we got to Carolina, I remember the color of the earth changing to red. The further south we got, the more the driver would shout every time you crossed a state line, and wake me up.

The bus would stop for lunch and dinner, and they had little counters in the depots where you could eat. South of the Mason-Dixon Line, black passengers would sit at the back of the bus. By the time you got to Alabama, the lunch counters and rest rooms were segregated; they had signs on, saying "Colored" and "White." If the depot was really small, the black people had to get their food from a serving hatch round the back.

When we got to Athens, Georgia, we pulled off to go for a rest stop. There was some kind of commotion, and the bus slowed down. The driver said, "Keep your seats, everybody, there won't be any trouble." Out of the window, I could see a couple of hand-held burning crosses and about seventeen Ku Klux Klansmen in robes and hoods. A couple of them got on the bus; they were looking for freedom riders. They looked around, didn't ask any questions, and got off. They were just trying to intimidate people, and I have to admit it was kind of scary. The bus driver said, "Sorry about that, folks. Just a local custom."

The early sixties were the worst time for the whole civil rights movement. The black people were trying to break free, and the white people were trying to stop them. So that was when it was at its worst, and the incident at Athens was my introduction to it.

I remember east of Biloxi miles and miles of deserted white sands with beautiful houses. Then we traveled into the country, and I'd never seen such abject poverty. If there was a hole in a wooden shack, they'd nail a metal tobacco sign over it.

Then the driver called out, "Louisiana state line," and I couldn't wait to get off the bus—by then, I'd been on it for forty hours. The driver called, "Yonder New Orleans!" You could see the tallest building in the city: it was the Hibernia National Bank. People used to come from all over the South just to see it. The bus stopped on Claiborne, and I saw a sign that said St. Philip Street. I knew I'd really arrived. I remember the whole city seemed to smell of cigar smoke.

I walked up Canal Street towards the river—didn't know where the hell I was—looking for a hotel. I kept stopping and looking around; it's a wonder the police didn't arrest me for loitering. I got to Camp Street, and somebody told me there were cheap hotels down there. There was a sign saying "Rooms by the week, real cheap." The lady showed me into a room, all dark wood, no windows, I dumped my bags and asked the way to the French Quarter. I crossed Canal and went looking for Bill Russell's record store on Chartres Street, but when I got there, it was all closed up. I went next door to the Alpine Restaurant to get something to eat and asked the waitress did she know Bill Russell. They sent me to the Bourbon House on Bourbon and St. Peter; Bill Russell's store was opposite where Preservation Hall is now.

I went there and banged on the door, it must have been ten in the morning by then. Nobody answered, and I banged on the door again. A voice came from inside: "Oh gee, the door's open! Do I have to come and answer it? I'm in the middle of doing something. Just walk in." I went in and said to the man, "Are you Bill Russell?" He said, "Yes." I said, "I'm a drummer from England. Do you mind if I sit down? I'm real tired—I just came in by bus from New York City." He asked me, "Did you see any of the New Orleans boys up there? I'm sorry I yelled at you, but I'm trying to scrape this bubble off this record." The store had an old fireplace and about nine record racks round the walls, some of which were empty. We sat and talked a while, and he said to me, "You must be a Baby Dodds fanatic. Take this." He went into the back of the store and came back with a bundle of papers with the title "The Baby Dodds Story"—it later appeared in his posthumously published book, *New Orleans Style*. So I happily sat there for about three hours reading, while he went on scraping at this bubble. I guess he was what you would call a perfectionist.

When I finished reading, I told him I thought it was great. He asked me, "Do you think you learned anything from it?" By then it was about one o'clock in the afternoon, and he said it was time for him to go to bed. I said, "Well, you go to bed early." And he replied, "I go to bed when I'm tired. If everybody had that kind of sense, the national economy wouldn't be in this mess." I knew I'd made a friend.

I asked him if I could come back and talk some more. He said, "Sure! There's another crazy Englishman in town—his name's Mike Slatter. Do you know him?" I didn't know Mike Slatter personally, but Bill said that I would, sooner or later.

I asked him where I could hear some New Orleans jazz, but he said it was very difficult. The Kid Thomas band had just lost their job across the river. He advised me against staying in Camp Street and told me I should move into the French Quarter. He said, "On your way back down Bourbon Street tonight, stop at the Paddock. [Alphonse] Picou just got through playing there, but Albert Burbank took the job."

The music at the Paddock was fast and furious. The band was Thomas Jefferson, Clement Tervalon, Albert Burbank,[9] Octave Crosby, Richard McLean, and a drummer called Bob Ogden. You bought a little bottle of beer, about the size of a Tabasco sauce bottle, and in those days, it cost two bucks! There were only about four people in the audience. After a couple of beers, I made it back to the hotel and fell asleep in my clothes.

The next morning, I walked over to Canal Street in search of breakfast, and found White Castle burgers—little tiny things, four for a dollar—they were really good. The lady asked me, "You wanna root beer?" I said "No, I never drink this early in the morning." She laughed—she though I was making a joke. She brought me one, and I've loved root beer ever since. I went back to Bill Russell's, and he played me some unissued American Music records. I think he was surprised by what I knew; he could tell by the questions I was asking.

The French Quarter in 1960 wasn't that different from how it is today, but in those days, Burgundy Street was the dividing line; white people hardly ever went beyond Burgundy. It was safe enough, but there just wasn't much reason to go over there. About a block past Orleans on Burgundy, going towards Esplanade Avenue, there was the Morning Star Baptist Church. I never had the nerve to go in, but I used to stand outside and hear the most beautiful music. On St. Peter and Burgundy, there was always an old man sitting there, wearing one of those big old high crown hats. His name was Tom Albert. He was very friendly; he would always greet me when I walked past. We got talking, and he told me the names of all these musicians he knew. He'd been a trumpet player himself.

I was still listening to one set at the Paddock every night, and Bill had said, "Tell Albert Burbank you're a friend of mine." I did, and Burbank invited me back to what he called the "lounge" in the intermission.

When he opened the door, it was more of a broom closet than a lounge. There was only space for three of the band to sit down. The other three had to stand up, but they weren't allowed to mix with the customers. In fact, the owner, Miss Valenti, came in and complained, saying, "What's this boy doing in here?" meaning me. Albert said, "He's making a recording with me, and we're talking business." I was in seventh heaven; all the musicians became very friendly. I remember telling Albert Burbank that I'd heard the records he'd made with Wooden Joe Nicholas, and he said he'd never heard them!

I don't know what he thought about Wooden Joe's playing, but the tonation, the attack, the placing of the notes, the feeling were all totally different from anything a European musician is trained to do. Joe was what you might call a soul cat, like John Casimir or Albert Jiles. They just come right out of the bag at you.

The band at the Paddock was the only band in town playing that kind of music; there was a very flourishing rhythm and blues scene, but I had come for the Dixieland. Let me clarify that: "Dixieland" was what all the New Orleans musicians called it, with the exception of George Lewis. I think his managers had told him that Dixieland was a white music, and he had taken that on board—I have never heard him call his music by that name.

There wasn't much crossover, but you would see R & B musicians playing in the brass bands. People like Wardell Quezergue, Melvin Lastie, and Ernest Poree. Even back then, the brass bands had aspects of fusion.

I was visiting Bill Russell in his store every day, and one day he told me that the other crazy Englishman, Mike Slatter, would be there the following day. I knew who Mike Slatter was; he'd recorded that great session with the Kid Thomas band—the one with "Coconut Island" and "Mama Inez." Anyway, he arrived at Bill's store in a black suit and a white shirt. He must have been at least six feet six inches tall, and he ducked his head as he came through the door. He spoke with an upper-crust English accent. He had fabulous enthusiasm for New Orleans music, but he was also a Ken Colyer fan. He didn't confuse the two things, but he put them both on the same level.

He told me that the Young Tuxedo Brass Band was playing a job across the river in Gretna on Sunday and invited me to go along. Mike was something of a fascist. In later years, I visited him in Chelsea, London, and he had pictures of Adolf Hitler on all the walls. In fact, he even answered the door dressed as a storm trooper—black riding pants, boots, and all that. It was weird: you'd be talking about Kid Thomas,[10] and he'd suddenly switch the conversation to solving the Jewish problem. It seems impossible that you could like a man who held views like that, but he was really a very nice guy. Strangely, in music he was absolutely not a racist, and all the New Orleans musicians really liked him.

One time, Mike said to Kid Thomas, "Tom, I heard that you're a painter. Last time I was in London, I saw this wonderful Chagall exhibition at the Tate Gallery." Thomas said something like, "Ain't that nice," and after Mike left, asked me what he'd been talking about. I explained that Mike had been talking about fine art. Thomas said, "I don't know anything about that. I'm a house painter." Yet he and Mike were really good friends. It was an outrageous combination.

Eventually, Mike Slatter had to leave England because of his fascist connections, and I think he moved to Spain. I'd love to see him again.

I'd been in New Orleans about three weeks, and the only band I'd heard was Albert Burbank's (which was billed as Octave Crosby's band) at the Paddock Lounge. They were pretty much playing "racehorse" music —everything was fast. It was what the management required, and it was pretty entertaining for a bunch of drunks from Columbus, Ohio; it's just that it didn't really entertain me. One Sunday afternoon around two o'clock, I was talking to Bill Russell in his store; the door opened and in came Slow Drag, Punch Miller, Kid Howard,[11] and Kid Sheik [George Cola]. I recognized all of them—I couldn't believe it. So they started talking, and I asked if I could take their pictures. Bill always rose to the occasion; he said, "Why not take a picture of Drag playing the guitar? He used to be a guitarist, so he wouldn't be faking." He went in the back and came out with a Spanish guitar with no strings and three trumpets. Only one of them had a mouthpiece. Punch took it and started to play "Tin Roof Blues." There was more soul in that than there was at the Paddock.

Another musician who came by the store a lot was the piano player Lester Santiago—they called him "Blackie." Sometimes he would come there drunk and sleep it off in Bill's chair. Bill didn't care. He was like St. Francis of Assisi; his hands were out to everyone. He was so polite it was unbelievable. I remember one time we went together to the funeral home on Claiborne and St. Philip. It was a really windy night, and as we passed a barroom, the door opened and a man staggered out backwards and fell down on the sidewalk. The light from the bar shone on the man's face, and Bill said, "Good evening, Mr. Morgan. Can I help you up?" He got him on his feet, helped him across the street, and rang a bell. A woman answered the door, thanked us, and took the drunk in. He was Isaiah Morgan, the trumpet player. But what struck me was the politeness of it all; that was Bill.

Around about that time, I went to this white people's dance and heard the first music that sounded like the real thing to me. The band was Kid

Sheik, Harold Dejan[12] on alto sax, John Smith on piano, and Fats Houston on drums. He wasn't much of a drummer, but when they started up "Song of the Islands," I knew this was what I'd come to New Orleans to hear. There was no vestige of commerciality about it; it was pure functional music.

I got to know Harold and Sheik pretty well. They were so hospitable and friendly they almost made Zutty Singleton seem standoffish by comparison. They had no idea that I was intending to make records or tour England with them. They had no idea that I would ever be able to do anything for them. They were just naturally nice, friendly people.

I decided that Camp Street was too far and too dangerous to stay there. So I moved to Tony's Spaghetti House, at 208 Bourbon Street. It was a big room upstairs over the restaurant. I got sick around then; it was cold, and I didn't have an overcoat. I asked the owner, Miss Josephine, if she had any kind of a cold cure. She was very nice. She walked down to the French Market to get a couple of lemons to make me a hot drink.

A few days later, I had been out somewhere with Kid Sheik, and I invited him to come back to my room for a drink, which he did. The next morning, Miss Josephine gave me a hell of a lecture: "Don't bring no colored people up here." I asked her why; I couldn't be horrible to her after her being so nice. She told me, "Look, I ain't prejudiced. A nigger's as good as I am, in my book. But I can't have you bringing them here. What will the customers think?" It was a revelation to me, how a basically nice woman could talk like that. There didn't seem any logic to it. A few months before I got to New Orleans, they'd just taken the segregating screens out of the buses, but most black people still sat at the back.

You very rarely saw black people on Bourbon Street in those days. If they did venture up there, especially if they looked at the strippers, it would really upset the cops. One especially nasty cop—I forget his name—would poke them hard in the small of the back with his billy stick. "C'mon, move along."

Mostly segregation only worked one way. Me and Emanuel Sayles once got thrown out of a black bar on our asses, but I honestly couldn't say if it was because of racial reasons or because we were drunk. Generally speaking, you couldn't go into a white place if you were with a friend or another musician and they were black and you were white. You could visit them at their houses, but if the police stopped you, you had to have proof you were going there on business. I used to carry a folded-up musicians' union contract in my pocket. Although if you were in a black neighborhood, they had mostly black cops, and they didn't care. I remember one white good cop, Officer O'Reilly. If you were playing with a mixed band, he would stand outside the building to make sure nobody gave you any trouble. Watching all this crazy stuff happening, you felt like saying to your black friends, "Listen. There is another part of the world where people don't care about this stuff." I never sensed any anti-white prejudice amongst musicians in those days.

The first musician I phoned for a chat was Clement Tervalon. He was real friendly, like everybody else. The next was Cié Frazier,[13] who invited me over to his place the next day. He lived on Onzaga Street. I went over there, and he was very friendly, but he wasn't much of a conversationalist. I asked if I could take his picture, and he asked me to wait a minute. He went in the back, came back with his drum kit, and set the whole thing up. It didn't occur to him that I would take his picture without his drums. His bass drum had a stripe on it, with the initials D.G. I asked him what the initials stood for, and he told me, "Damn good!" Turned out it was really the initials of the drum's previous owner, but I don't think Cié ever rubbed them off. He played for me. I had my own concert right there in the house.

After about an hour, his wife appeared. That was typical; if you visited a black musician's home, the wives would stay out of the way, at least to start with. Like at Jim Robinson's house, his wife, Pearl, would cook for you, serve the food and then go away. Don't ask me why, I never understood it.

Back in England there had been a publication specializing in New Orleans jazz called *Eureka* magazine. It was totally uncommercial, didn't accept advertisements, and only ran for seven issues, published at irregular intervals. At one point, the editorial board consisted of me, Stuart McMillan, and a guy called Graham Russell. He was one of the unsung enthusiastic heroes. He was a big tall guy, all torso and head, with very short legs. He knew more about New Orleans jazz—the records and the musicians—in the fifties than most people do today. He lived with his mother in Maida Vale in London, and we were very good friends. I would go to his house and listen to records. He very rarely came out. He was a commercial artist, and he did all the design work on *Eureka* magazine. But he was a perfectionist, and it took forever to get an issue out.

He had written to me when I was in Canada, asking if he could come out to New Orleans when I got there. He came towards the latter part of my stay and moved in with me at 208 Bourbon Street. There was only one bed; one of us had to sleep on the floor.

Graham was interested in collecting information on Kid Howard. That work was later published in *Storyville* magazine; even today, it's the best thing that's been done on Howard. He was a controversial figure; he had very conservative musical tastes, but he knew what he was talking about.

He suffered from narcolepsy, a medical condition that makes you suddenly fall asleep at odd times—it used to be called sleeping sickness. His death was strange. Some people say he committed suicide, other people say he fell asleep. Either way, he fell under a London subway train. I've never thought of committing suicide myself; I've always been too busy.

I went up to a church parade uptown with a guy called Carey Tate. One of the trumpet players was Alvin Alcorn, who I knew of before I came to New Orleans. I got talking to him and introduced him to Carey Tate. Alvin stuck his hand out and said, "Alcorn!" Carey said, "Gee, I'm pleased to meet you, Mr. Corn."

Alvin was really friendly. I remember he introduced me to Bill Matthews and Andrew Jefferson, who were playing trombone and snare drum, respectively. I asked him what time the job would start, and he said, "We've been waiting for the man. Here he comes now." Down the street came this character with an alto saxophone. Alvin said to him, "This boy's over here from England" and the man stuck out his hand and said, "Harold 'Duke' Dejan." It was the start of a friendship that lasted until he died.

Harold took over, but not in a nasty way. He got them lined up, sent for the organizer, called all the numbers. It wasn't even his band. Before he got there, they'd just been standing around. After the job, he asked me where I was staying and offered me a ride back. During the ride, he asked me what I was doing in New Orleans. I said I was gathering information and hoped to organize a couple of recording sessions. He asked me if I knew any musicians. I told him I didn't—I hadn't been in town long enough. He said, "We'll soon put that right. I get off work tomorrow at quarter to five. Meet me at Lykes Shipping Office." I asked him what we were going to do, and he said, "Oh, we'll think of something!"

He was there on time, and he took me to meet Alex Bigard, whom everyone called "Alec." He banged on the door and shouted, "Alec, open up, you damn fool! What the hell you doing in there?" That was his way. Alec was a strange cat; I've never heard a drummer like him before or since. It was probably the oldest style of drumming.

Harold told him to set up his drums, and he said that they were in the kitchen. Harold said, "I don't care if they're in the shithouse! Set them up, man! What the hell's the matter with you?"

Harold went out to the car and got his alto, and I got a concert for about an hour—saxophone and drums—in Alec's kitchen. I've got a picture of it. I remember Alec played a drum solo, leaned forward, and said, "How you like that? I used to play that solo with Manuel Perez."

The next musician Harold introduced me to was George Guesnon.[14] You could walk to his place on 1012 North Roman. Both of them were intent on telling the story of the music of their people. George Guesnon was the most eccentric person I've ever met. You'd love him, you'd hate him, and you'd love him again, all in the space of about five minutes. Normally, I hate banjos. To me, it's not a musical instrument; it ought to be put up there with the glockenspiel. I'd rather work with a chainsaw than a banjo—it's more musical, and it's got a volume control. At the time, banjo was reckoned to be the "authentic" instrument by the white "revivalists"—guitar was supposed to be dreadful. It was like the prejudice they had against saxophones. It got so that musicians like Paul Barnes would play a job on saxophone and not tell anyone. He realized the white pressure on him to play "authentic" New Orleans music, which meant playing only clarinet. Emanuel Sayles was another one. He would never suggest to anyone that he should play guitar.

George Guesnon was primarily a banjoist. He did double on four-string tenor guitar, which is tuned the same as a banjo. He was the only banjo player whose music I loved. He had such a fantastic beat. He was inspirational to me, but he had his detractors. He lived in this little house; it only had around two feet of sidewalk. He came to the door—he was a big, burly man with a lot of gold teeth—and said, "Hey, Harold! Who is this boy?" Harold said, "He's come here to learn about New Orleans jazz. He's going around talking to a lot of colored musicians." You didn't call people "black" at that time.

George said, "Come on in, you're welcome. You interested in our music? I can tell you about it." He started telling me about John Marrero and people who were just names in books to me. He knew the sort of thing I wanted to know. We had to leave after a short time because Harold had to go somewhere, and George said, "Come back tomorrow." I used to go and see him about three times a week and sit and talk with him. He didn't have a car, but he would invite people to his house for me to meet.

That's how I met Jimmy "Kid" Clayton, the trumpet player. He was a little guy with nothing but gold teeth and a pink scar on his mouth from the pressure of the trumpet mouthpiece. He was a strange one. I've heard him play some of the worst trumpet and some of the best. He and George were great friends, although George carried a bullet in his leg that Clayton had put there—had it until the day he died. George's personality was quirky, to say the least. I remember going to his place just after some little black girls had been killed in Mississippi. He answered the door, looked very stern, and said, "I ought to just kill you. I don't think you'd better come in today. Look at this." And he showed me the newspaper report. He said, "You did this!" I said, "Me? I'm here in New Orleans. I don't know anything about this. Why the hell are you blaming me? I'm not coming back here!" He changed straight away, saying, "Oh man, don't go. I didn't mean anything. I don't want you not to come back." He was a very lonely man; he lived alone with a little dog he called Goose. He had run his wife and daughter off with his volatility.

He wrote poetry, would play the banjo at the drop of a hat. One time when I was round there, he said, "Look. I buried a tape in a hole in the wall. But I've decided to bring it out and play it for you." There was a hole in the wall about the size of a teacup that he'd made with an ice pick or a penknife or something where he'd buried this tape. He put it on, and a voice said, "This is George Guesnon, speaking to you from beyond the grave. I want to tell you the real story of jazz, which I could not tell while these cats were still living." He names a lot of musicians saying they were no good. He was a very sensitive man. If you weren't pacifying him, you were scolding him, and if you weren't doing either of those, you were learning from him. He was a tireless teacher. He was a gambler—he always lost. He didn't spend much on clothes; he seemed to only own one pair of pants. Wardrobe wasn't his thing.

He invited Israel Gorman to his house to meet me, and loads of other people. He worked at Preservation Hall when it opened, but he didn't stay long. When you came to share out the tips money there, you had to make one share for the hall itself. One particular night when his band was playing there, one of the Jaffes said to him, "Don't forget to make the share for the Preservation Hall." George just threw all the money on the floor, and said, "There! Take the goddamn lot. I ain't coming back here no more!" He walked out and never went back. He was very proud.

Emanuel Sayles had just moved back to town from Chicago. Word soon got around that if you wanted a smooth-running recording session or gig, you should hire Sayles and not George. But I would never hire anyone over George Guesnon. You could set a metronome by him. I've never known anyone like him. I was very sad when he died—it was a gap that was never filled.

Harold Dejan was simply the nicest man I've ever met. He was totally devoid of jealousy or pettiness. He was going to take me to Mississippi to meet a banjo player called Harry Fairconnetue. Harry got sick, and we didn't go. But Harold got him to write his life story and mailed it to me in England! He'd do anything for you, and he didn't want anything from you. He liked everybody, he had a heart like a buffalo's ass until the day he died.

Most of those old-style musicians had never heard themselves play, and that was the reason many of them wanted to make recordings. It's easy to forget that.

Of these musicians I met, Harold Dejan, Kid Sheik, and George Guesnon were real friends, and they were to remain so. The rest of the people were friendly towards me, very kind and considerate at all times.

The first time I played in New Orleans was when I sat in one night with the Paul Barbarin[15] band on Bourbon Street. Paul was very friendly; he was also still musically very active then. He was much less of what you would call a stylist than Cié Frazier or Alec Bigard. The band were just there for one appearance. Paul said to me, "Come and play." It wasn't as simple as he had made it sound. You were crossing the line in two ways. Firstly, you were crossing a personal line by playing with people you regarded as heroes. Secondly, you were crossing the color line. You didn't mix the cream with the coffee in those days, and if the cops had stopped by, there was a good chance you could all wind up in jail. So I said to Paul, "Are you sure it will be OK?" and he reassured me that it would.

I started off by playing four beats to the measure; it was what I was used to doing. Kid Howard turned round and hollered, "Play two beats!" Frog Joseph shouted, "Don't play the bass drum that way!" Paul said to them afterwards, "There's no sense yelling and screaming at this boy. He'll learn." But I learned a lot just from the yelling and screaming. What they wanted was the first and third beats on the bass drum. It took me a long time to learn to do that correctly, but it got a lot easier when I took lessons with Cié Frazier; I could make syncopations with it.

Another big influence on my drum style was Alfred Williams. All the kit he used was a big twenty-eight-inch bass drum, a snare drum (both single tension), and a sock cymbal that sounded like a gong. But he could swing a band more than anyone.

A while later, I went up to a job with Harold near Tulane. I think it was part of the university. Harold had hired two drummers by mistake, Alec Bigard and Alfred Williams. He didn't send either of them home; he paid both of them. Then he told them, "Come on, let this boy play now" (meaning me). I couldn't believe it—when I played, neither of them got down off the stage, they just sat there on either side of me, each of them about a foot away. Both were coaching me as I went along—it was a job trying to concentrate. Luckily, the music was a bit wild, and didn't require too much finesse from the drums. So it was easier to play with two drumming legends shouting advice at the same time. But they both said the same thing, "Don't be scared of the bass drum."

When I came to New Orleans for the first time, you couldn't find a bad drummer. There was no point in looking in the Yellow Pages under *B*. The less proficient were people like Albert Francis, George Williams, or Fats Houston. But at least they had a beat.

I want to talk about Dick Allen, because he was a prime mover in my life in New Orleans. I can't remember where I first met him. He was very different from Bill Russell. I had saved $2,000 working in Canada, and my father had sent me $1,000. I walked round wearing $3,000 in a money belt. I couldn't open a bank account because I was in the U.S. illegally. Eventually, I asked Bill Russell if I could leave it with him for safe keeping. He asked me what I was intending to do with all that money, and I told him I wanted to record a couple of sessions and do some interviews. I knew he was doing interviews, so I asked him how it worked.

He told me that he and Dick Allen were working together on an interview program at Tulane University, funded by the Ford Foundation. They'd done a stack of interviews, and they were still doing them. I had people in mind to interview, but there was no point in us both interviewing the same people. So I decided to concentrate on drummers because that was my instrument, starting with the ones I had met in the preceding few weeks.

I'd talked to Cié Frazier, Alfred Williams, and Alec Bigard, along with a few other people. Bill said, "Well, if you give a copy to the Tulane Archive, you can use our Ampex 600." That was the state-of-the-art machine—a big, heavy thing it was. He asked if he could attend the interviews, partly to look after the tape recorder, but mainly because he was just interested. I told him I'd be very pleased if he would come.

Up at Tulane, I think Bill was the curator and Dick Allen was the assistant curator. I mentioned that I also wanted to do a couple of recording sessions, and Bill said, "Golly, there's nothing worth recording here—you'd be throwing your money away."

I told him I wanted to record Kid Sheik, because no one ever had. Bill had recorded one type of music, which a lot of people criticize him for. They would say that he only recorded Bunk Johnson and bands that he personally liked. I mean, the man put his own money up to finance those recordings and lugged his big old acetate recording machine. Why shouldn't he record what he liked? I'd never criticize anything to do with Bill.

Anyway, he suggested that I discuss my recording project with Dick Allen, and that's what I did—I think we met at the Bourbon House. He was more positive; I remember him saying, "Russell's talking nonsense. There's always something worth recording." I thought straight away that he was my kind of guy.

I liked both Bill Russell and Dick Allen, but I got the impression that they didn't particularly like each other. A few days later, I went up to Tulane to find Bill, because his store was closed. Dick was there, and I asked if Bill was around. "No," he said, in a derogatory way. "He's never here. He's probably out recording interviews." I mean, Dick wouldn't have had that job if it hadn't been for the interview program.

Nevertheless, we struck up an instant friendship. In some ways, he was a more friendly guy than Bill, but he didn't have the single-mindedness that Bill and I shared. Both of them were willing to help me, but they were very different.

Dick was basically a lazy man. He could have written the book that Sam Charters wrote.[16] But he didn't. In later years, he began to believe his own publicity. If you asked him for some information, he would say, "The information you require is at Tulane University on Tape 24F, which is the interview with . . ." That's what cooled our friendship finally. But Dick was a good guy, he was fun.

There was nothing lazy about Bill. He used to walk everywhere; he used to figure that that would make you live longer. If he had to interview Kid Thomas, who lived on Wagner Street in Algiers, he would lug that big Ampex 600 machine over the Canal Street ferry and then lug it back. He would never take a cab.

In later years, I went up to the John Reid Collection in Little Rock, Arkansas, to pick up the Burnell Santiago recordings. They wouldn't let me take the records away with me. They insisted on sending them to New Orleans on the Arkansas Gas plane, which flew down to Louisiana twice a week to pick up mail. I had to stay up all night copying them—they had to be returned the following day. When I got home, I called Bill and said the copies had been made. He asked if I could take them to him so he could hear them. I was exhausted; I told him I'd bring them to him in the morning. He said, "Can't you bring them here now?" I said, "Bill, it's 4:00 a.m.!" He asked, "Does that matter?" So I went down there. This was when he was in his eighties—he never lost his phenomenal enthusiasm.

I had to make a choice to start my own record label. I wanted to record New Orleans jazz as it was at the time I went there. I didn't want to tell musicians what tunes they should play or who they should have in the band. Other people did.

Anyway, I went to Kid Sheik and told him that one of my reasons for coming to New Orleans was to record him, because no one else had. He wasn't a phenomenal trumpet player, but he was another soul cat, like Brother Cornbread[17] or Wooden Joe or John Casimir. I asked who he would like to use, and he told me, "Harold Dejan." That pleased me greatly, because Harold and I had become good friends by then. He also asked for his childhood friend Eddie Summers on trombone, who hadn't been recorded either. He suggested John Smith on piano, Slow Drag on bass, Alec Bigard on drums, and Fred Minor on banjo. I was more than satisfied with that—it was exactly the sort of thing I wanted to do.

Also, I had become friendly with Emile Barnes.[18] I loved his clarinet playing and I wanted to record him. He wasn't in the union, so I had to make him an offer, because my money was shrinking. He said, "Yeah, of course I'll do it, man. I like you—you're a nice fella." It was common knowledge that he had killed two men when he was younger. By the time I knew him, he was old. He was down to his last two teeth, but he was very strong. You thought he would never die.

When you went to his house, which was in a rough neighborhood, he'd insist on walking you to the bus. It was about four blocks. The centerpiece of his living room was a TV set with no screen. He said the only person who knew how to run a band was Artie Shaw. I said, "Oh, did you like his playing?" Emile said, "I dunno about that, but at least he had the sense to stand in front of the band with his clarinet." When he walked you to the bus, all the local ruffians would defer to him: "Good evening, Mr. Barnes. Nice to see you out." They feared him. He would just grunt back at them.

Anyway, I told him to pick his men for the session, and he chose Eddie Richardson on trumpet. I asked him if we could rehearse, and he said, "Of course. Let's go over to Richardson's and talk about it." We took the bus over there the next day. Richardson lived on Jane Alley, opposite were Louis Armstrong had lived. He agreed straight away and suggested Sammy Penn as the drummer and Joe James on piano. They were good choices, but I pointed out that there could be a problem because both of those men were in the musicians' union. Emile got real agitated and said, "The union? I'll fix that right now! Richardson, where's your phone?" He made a call, and I heard him say "Cottrell? This is Milé Barnes. I'm going to record with two of your boys out of the union, Penn and James, next Saturday. That's alright with you ain't it? OK. Thank you very much, Cottrell." Louis Cottrell was president of the union at that time, and I hadn't yet met him. But with Milé it was a bit like Al Capone calling and saying he was coming round for tea—you didn't tell him no.

So then I had two recording sessions set up, and I knew how much money I had left in my budget. I was paying five dollars for interviews, and the first one I did was Joe Watkins,[19] on January 20. I also interviewed Kid Sheik, Emanuel Sayles, Alfred Williams, and Cié Frazier.

Joe Watkins was in bad shape; he really needed the five dollars. First his wife and then his little dog had died, so he was sick and all on his own. He lived above 832 North Galvez Street. The buses used to stop there. Joe's leg was bandaged up; he could barely walk. All the black people feared going into the colored ward of Charity Hospital. It was like nobody there gave a shit about them. You died of one of two things, "internal or external."

I had seen him with George Lewis in England, and I couldn't believe I was actually sitting in his house talking to him. His right name was Mitchell Watson. I got to be very friendly with him. He never met my mother, but he asked if I minded if he wrote to her; he liked me, so he figured she must be a nice person. They must have exchanged about twenty letters. Every time I went there, he would talk about when he would start playing again. I could see that he probably never would, but the thought of it kept him going. It was kind of sad.

One day he said to me, "Look. I hate to ask you this, but you can see I'm in a bad way. Could you lend me fifty dollars?" That was the first time anyone had asked me for anything, but I could look in that man's eyes and I knew he really needed that money. So I agreed, and he offered to pay me back a dollar a month, which he did, until he died.

I mean, he had nothing. He couldn't leave the house—his leg was so bad it couldn't hold him. Something a lot of people don't know about him was that he would never sing a song without having the lyrics in front of him. He had a little songbook that he could carry around. He was what we call a southpaw drummer—left hand, left foot. But Jesus Christ, what a beat!

When it came time to make the recording session with Emile Barnes, he had got sick the night before, but he didn't tell me. So his playing on that record is about 20 percent as good as he had been at the rehearsal.

The Kid Sheik rehearsal took place at Slow Drag's house. Even though Drag's wife, Annie, was a piano player, the piano sounded as if it hadn't been tuned for about fifty years. The room was about fifteen feet square. It sounded terrifically loud, but I just let them go.

I had visited Sheik one afternoon to agree what tunes to record. He suggested "Song of the Islands," "Sheik of Araby," and "Down in Honky-Tonk Town." He knew exactly what he wanted to do. He was a simple man, but he certainly wasn't simple minded. He was just a product of his society.

The union sent an official to oversee the session, and on this occasion they sent Melvin Lastie. He was a modern trumpet player, but he loved old-style Dixieland music.

After I left New Orleans the first time, I wrote this account of the session during the journey home.

Sheik's Swingsters

I had always imagined Kid Sheik, George Cola, to be a good player, but until I reached New Orleans, I had never heard him play. My first hearing, even though only on a tape at Tulane University, proved to be all I needed before confirming my thoughts on recording him.

On this first hearing Sheik was playing with Charles Love on a session that was recorded by Walter Eysselinck. After hearing the tape through twice I decided that Sheik ought to be recorded leading his own band. I was busy for the next few days, but on January 19, [1961,] Dick Allen and I went over the Industrial Canal to Sheik's home and lined up the whole thing.

Sheik greeted us at the door and showed us into the main room, where, after looking through his collection of photographs, we brought up what we had come to say. Sheik seemed really pleased at the idea, and we asked him who he would like to use. He replied, "My regular men, of course." So we settled on Harold Dejan, Eddie Summers, John Smith, but even a search in Sheik's union book for John Smith seemed fruitless. Harold was a sax player, and Sheik was pleased when we didn't want Harold to get his clarinet out for the session.

We didn't decide on the songs that day, although Sheik said it wouldn't be his band if we didn't record "Song of the Islands," his theme song. Dick Allen said it was imperative to have them play "The Sheik of Araby" too. A couple of tunes like "Rose Leaf Rag" and "Confessin'" were suggested, but I asked Sheik to work out a list of songs by next week. We decided on a Tulane hall for the session, and the date would be right after Carnival. We left Sheik's place with a feeling of satisfaction.

The very next day while in Bill Russell's shop I met Sheik. He had been at work on choosing the songs and his little list showed fifteen numbers, none of which were hackneyed standards. He told me these were the kind of numbers he played at a dance. I knew I would get along fine with him running the band.

The next two weeks I was busy with other sessions and interviews, but every now and then I saw Sheik, who told me he was ready
anytime and for me not to worry as everything would turn out fine.
Around February 1 I saw by the way my money was running out that
I would have to record the band before Carnival, as it didn't look as
though I would be around after. I arranged with Sheik a rehearsal for
the following Sunday and tried to get a hall. This proved impossible,
so we settled on Slow Drag's little home on St. Ann Street.

Meanwhile, news had come through that Sheik had a dance job on
the Saturday, so I phoned him for the details, hoping for a preview of
the band's sound. I had not heard them play yet. Unfortunately this
particular job called for only four pieces. Sheik, Harold, and Smitty
were to play with Fats Houston on drums.

Sheik picked me up around eight at Bill Russell's, and we picked up
the other men en route, arriving at the place in time for them to set up.
After their first number, "Song of the Islands," I knew the recording
would be a success. After the dance we all went home to bed, as the
rehearsal was set for the next day.

After watching a parade for the Corner Club the next morning,
I drove back to Drag's house with Fred Minor, who happened to be
playing trumpet in a brass band. When we arrived, only Bigard's
drums were there. Sheik arrived, followed by Bigard, Drag, Minor,
and Noone Johnson. Harold arrived and remembered he had forgotten
to pick up Smitty. We still didn't know his right name yet. After a half
hour everyone turned up except Summers. He had been on a parade
all day and had been drinking heavily. However, he finally made it,
and the band went through the fifteen songs one by one. Although the
piano could not be put in tune with the instruments, that New Orleans
beat and sound quickly became apparent. After the rehearsal Sheik and
I picked out five songs for the recording.

The date was now set for Sunday, February 12, at 2:00 p.m., but in
the course of the next week, so many things happened. Picou died,
and all New Orleans was upside down with the funeral arrangements.
Carnival was being prepared for, and to top it all Harold had to play
a parade on February 12. After about three trips out to Tulane we finally got the day changed to Saturday at 2:00 p.m. Two days before
the session something else came up, and the time had to be changed

again. This time the recording was set for Saturday, February 11, at 4:00 p.m.

In the afternoon of the eleventh, George Lewis and Kid Thomas were playing across the street from Bill's shop at a wedding, and Sheik turned up complete in his tuxedo. This was really his day, and I think he was just a little nervous.

At around 3:00 p.m. I left the wedding and went to collect the photographer. After about half an hour we managed to get away in his car for Tulane, stopping on the way to pick up a fifth of bourbon for the band.

We arrived at McAlister Hall at exactly 4:00 p.m. and found the band on stage warming up. Fred Minor hadn't arrived yet, though. McAlister Hall is part of Tulane University; there is a long crescent-shaped stage about five feet high and rows of seats to the rear of the stage where the orchestra sit. From the stage the place extends for several hundred yards to the rear of the hall. There is a huge circle at the rear, and the wings extend both sides.

After the band had played "Gloryland" and a "Lord, Lord, Lord" to warm up and a balance was found, Sheik kicked off and played for all they were worth. Things went pretty smoothly, but in one number Minor, the banjo player, broke a string. This was rectified in time for him to take a solo on the release, however. In about two hours they played the "Song of the Islands" theme song, and it was all over. Sheik and his band were on tape at last.

That night in Bill's store, Sheik, Harold, Drag, and the union man, Sidney Montague, listened to the playbacks, and I think they all knew how their combined enthusiasm, recording for the first time, had made this a good session of their city's music.

The Riverside recordings started in the January of my first visit. Herbert Friedwald came to town. He was a New York Jewish lawyer. He'd become involved in the local scene through Bill Russell and Dick Allen in the days when he had studied law at Tulane University. He was an eccentric kind of guy, always wore the same box-back corduroy coat and talked out of the side of his mouth in a New York kind of way. If you didn't know him, you'd have thought he was a slick operator. I met him at the Bourbon House with Dick Allen, and he told us his plan. Bill Grauer, joint owner of Riverside Records, was going to come down to New Orleans.

He intended to audition the Kid Thomas band with Emile Barnes. If that went well, they intended to record seven bands. So I heard as much great music in that week as I did in the rest of my first visit.

The audition for the Thomas band took place at a hall we jokingly called the Royal Garden. It was on the corner of Royal Street and Ursuline, just a big empty gallery belonging to Larry Borenstein. Riverside didn't want to use Manuel Paul, who was the regular saxophone player in the Kid Thomas band. It was the usual outside prejudice against having saxophones in that kind of music.

I went along with Herb to the audition. It seemed to me that the band took forever to set up. They had Milé Barnes, Manuel Sayles, Joe James, Sammy Penn, Louis Nelson,[20] Twat Butler, and Kid Thomas. After what seemed an eternity, they were ready. But Bill Grauer was sitting there expressionless, and the band just sat there too, doing nothing. No one asked them to start or hurry it up or anything. Then, without any discussion or warning, Thomas banged his foot on the floor, and they launched into "Hindustan." I've never heard music like that in my life. It was so powerful the walls seem to move back two feet. I thought it would bring the police from Canal Street.

I had met Thomas before this, at Raymond Burke's record shop on Bourbon Street, down by Esplanade. I'd met Joe "Twat" Butler, the bass player, too. He had been arrested once for driving the wrong way across the Mississippi River bridge. Most people couldn't have got up the off ramp, but he had found a way.

Sammy Penn, the drummer, was a real easygoing man, but I saw him play with George Lewis at Preservation Hall. George upset him some kind of way, and Penn just turned his chair and the whole drum outfit round and played the rest of the set facing the wall.

Joe James, the piano player, was Thomas's favorite in the band. When he died, it was like the beginning of the end. They could go on jobs, just the two of them, Thomas and Joe, and satisfy the people.

Bill Grauer left town after the audition. Herbert said to me that he was going to Jim Robinson's house that night and did I want to come. I said sure, and he went round to 933 Marais Street. Herb had brought a couple of Sam Morgan records that Jim had recorded in 1927. He asked Jim if there were any good songs he had played with that band that they didn't record, and Jim said, "'Whenever You're Lonesome, Telephone Me.'"

He wanted to use Louis Cottrell on clarinet. Herbert only knew him as president of the musicians' union, so he thought it would be a shrewd political move to use him. They settled on Ernie Cagnolatti for trumpet, Alfred Williams on drums, Slow Drag on bass, and Guesnon on banjo.

It all happened so fast, and the jazz fans knew it was the most significant set of recordings since Bill Russell's American Music series. Besides which, Riverside was a major recording company. They sent down their main man after Bill Grauer left town: Chris Albertson, who later wrote a book on Bessie Smith. He was the A and R [artists and repertoire] man. They had fixed to record at the Jeunes Amis Hall, next door to Albert Burbank's house.

Around that time, Alphonse Picou died. He was the last of the real old-timers, and it turned the town upside down. It was the biggest funeral New Orleans had ever seen. I followed behind the Eureka Brass Band at the funeral. The leader, Percy Humphrey, was out of town, so Kid Sheik led the band. I think that was the second time I heard them. By then, a lot of the Eureka's men had passed on. They had lost, in a short space of time, Red Clark, the tuba player; Sunny Henry, the trombonist; Reuben Roddy on alto sax; and trumpet player Willie Pajeaud. Another trumpet player, Eddie Richardson, had some kind of breakdown and quit the band. So they brought in replacements: either Wilbert Tillman or Noone Johnson on tuba, Willie Humphrey on alto, Chicken Henry on trombone, Peter Bocage and Kid Sheik on trumpets.

That two-week period was fantastic. After so long being musically starved, everything was happening at once: the Riverside sessions, my own recording sessions, Picou's funeral—it was incredible.

I used to walk over to attend the Riverside recordings. Union scale at that time was sixty-eight dollars a man, double for leader. Cottrell was president of the union; Alvin Alcorn was vice president. Officials were Sidney Montague, Melvin Lastie, and Sidney Cates. One of the officials would attend recording sessions to make sure you didn't record more than fifteen minutes of music. This was strictly enforced. That was what they called a half session. They figured you'd get four numbers out of it. You were only allowed three takes of the same tune. More than that, and you're into overtime. As I got to know the union people, they got to be a bit more relaxed. They could see I wasn't making money out of it: I looked like a ragbag. But the Riverside people circumvented all of that by simply paying union scale.

In those days, a lot of people would show up on a recording session to see what was going on. It was a major event. As well as the hardcore fans, there was a whole gang of photographers who were documenting the music in their own way. Riverside had hired Ralston Crawford to do the cover shots for their records, but there was also Lee Friedlander, Florence Mars—they were a different crowd from us. They had discovered that old black musicians in their houses were a photographer's dream as far as social documentation goes. To do this work, they had to cross a line, which in some senses was a legal line.

All of this happened at a time when hardly anybody gave a rat's ass about New Orleans music or musicians. The local attitude was "It's just nigger music. We don't want to listen to that shit!" Things started changing when civil rights came in, and today you've got New Orleans musicians touring the world's concert stages. Back in 1961, many of us knew the change would come.

Everybody who attended those Riverside sessions has got their own stories, but these are the ones that spring to mind. For the Jim Robinson band, they brought in a record player and played the Sam Morgan record of "Mobile Stomp" for the band to listen to. Because the union allowed you to make three takes of everything, Chris Albertson decided that that's what he wanted.

Sweet Emma Barrett came to her session without her bells. I guess she thought they wouldn't be needed on a recording session. But they were, and the recording was held up while she went home for the bells.

On the Billie[21] and De De [Pierce][22] session, Albert Jiles, the drummer, was standing in the doorway, and they just started playing. He had to come running in to join in with them.

Before Jim Robinson used Louis Cottrell, a lot of people hadn't realized that he played clarinet. But he surprised them all, and they set up a trio session featuring him, with Manuel Sayles on guitar and Slow Drag on bass. Halfway through the session, they had to send Drag home; he couldn't cut some of the chord changes, and they hired McNeal Breaux.

The Peter Bocage session was spectacular and produced some of the most beautiful New Orleans music ever. Just listen to Pete playing violin on "Purple Rose of Cairo"—it's the stuff that dreams are made of, with Louis Cottrell playing the beautiful clarinet obligato.

But that kind of sound didn't fit a lot of people's preconceptions of what New Orleans jazz should sound like. In later years Peter Bocage was working one night a week at Preservation Hall. Once when I was there, I heard proprietor Allen Jaffe say to him, "Pete, could you play a little less violin?" Pete said to him, "You don't want the violin, my boy, you don't want me. I was there when jazz started, and you're telling me how to play? I won't even bother to bring my band here." Jaffe climbed down pretty quickly.

Pete was a strong character—you didn't tell him what to do—and all the musicians respected him. I was at a recording session where they had Cié on drums; Pete shouted to him, "Don't be beating so loud on those drums, boy!"

He was an authority that all the musicians respected. He once said to me, "I like Louis [Cottrell]. He's a nice boy; he's got very conservative habits. He don't smoke, don't drink, and don't fool with loose women."

The Riverside recordings were the first time I heard Alfred Williams play the drums. He was known as "the clock." Never sped up or slowed down, and played very simply. He played with the sock cymbal closed, and just opened it up on the last chorus. His style was the complete opposite of, say, Baby Dodds. His career went back to playing with Manuel Perez. They called him "Black Alfred," and he was the nicest, friendliest guy you could meet. Always joking, always laughing. In fact, when I was first looking for a drum teacher, I wanted to go to Alfred. He said to me in his soft-spoken way, "Man, I don't even know what I'm doing myself. How the hell can I teach you?"

When Riverside had recorded the Kid Thomas band, that was the end of the project. Thomas didn't want to wait to listen to the playbacks. Everyone had to sign for their recording fee; there was a little pay desk set up. When they asked Thomas to sign, he stormed out of the hall and left his money behind. Herb Friedwald had to take it over to his wife later.

To give you an idea of what a big deal the Riverside recordings were, when OKeh, Columbia, or Victor had come to New Orleans, they'd recorded about six numbers each in a two-day visit. But here was a major record company recording everything. Herb Friedwald did a magnificent job.

* * *

I was doing documentary work, and also trying to improve as a musician. There was all this fabulous drumming going on all around me, so I wanted to pick a drum teacher. After Alfred turned me down, I went to Cié Frazier and said, "Look, I'd like you to teach me to play the drums." He said, "You already play the drums, I've heard you. But I'm not going to teach you if you just want to play like me. I'm not wasting my time with that." Anyway, he agreed to do it and fixed the fee at one dollar per lesson. He was doing me a big favor. We couldn't do it at his house—his wife couldn't have stood the noise—so we decided to use Bill Russell's store. The lessons were once a week, and we used one set of drums between us. Bill asked if he could tape the lessons, and those tapes are lodged at Tulane archive. Cié said, "The best thing I can teach you is what to play in a dance band."

What he taught me was how to play in different times: three-four, two-four, six-eight, and so on. I learned to play polkas, waltzes, mazurkas. He would say, "Play a continuous roll on the snare. Now, hum any waltz you want, and put the bass drum beats in. The bass drum should make the third and first beats." To this day, I always play waltzes that way. Anything I didn't grasp, he made me work until I did grasp it.

Towards the end of my stay, my money ran out. Cié insisted on keeping up the lessons, even though I couldn't pay him. I protested that he couldn't do it for nothing, and he said, "I'm doing it for nothing anyway—ain't but a dollar a lesson." He just made a joke out of it. I guess he must have thought I was an apt student.

I can read and write music, very slowly, but I can't read drum music. Because I wanted to be a band leader, writing music was a means of communicating with the other musicians. There wasn't much point in writing parts for myself—I knew what I was going to play.

A lot of people were scared of Cié. You didn't argue with him; he carried a mattress needle in his jacket—it was about a foot of sharpened steel. I don't know that he'd have ever used it on anyone. I certainly never heard about anything like that. But both Sheik and Albert Warner told me that when they went up to Cleveland with Cié, they were in an elevator after the job. Cié said, "Man, that was a killer. I thought the gig would never end." Warner said, "I thought it was OK. I could go back down there and do the whole thing again." Cié just exploded: "Motherfucker! I'm going to stick you with my needle." But he didn't. It was all for nothing.

Cié could get a little agitated, but he would do anything for you if he liked you, and he liked most people. He was completely unaffected by the racial thing. I loved him; he looked out for me.

Years later, when I was leading the Legends of Jazz, we did a job up in Minnesota. Cié came to the gig; he was up there with the Preservation Hall touring band. In the intermission, I asked him if he would play with my band, just so I could say he had played with us. It sounded fabulous to me, and when I went back on the stage, I asked the band how they had enjoyed his playing. Andrew Blakeney[23] said, "Man, he doesn't know what he's doing. He's too damn loud." Joe Darensbourg[24] said, "He can't get his beat together." Ed Garland said, "That man's hopeless! I was praying for you to come back."

Back in 1961, I decided I wanted to film Cié and Alfred Williams. They were the two top drummers for me. I decided to get them to do the two marches "High Society" and "Maryland, My Maryland." The film makes up part of the Baby Dodds video on American Music. Here was the difference between them: Cié sang the tunes to himself as he played. But Alfred couldn't play without someone else providing a lead, so Kid Sheik came and sang the melodies for him.

If you catch me playing on a real good night, you'll get some idea of how the great drummers sounded when I first came to New Orleans.

I did the Emile Barnes recording session first, because it was the smaller of the two. In order to make a ten-inch vinyl record, you needed six numbers. The union allowed you to do four. I would always do a blues, and we'd do two takes in different keys. This session was non-union, so it was easier.

We'd selected some nice numbers, including "Surrender," which I've never heard before, or since. Eddie Richardson came up with it. Emile suggested "Now Is the Hour," which I still find very moving. It was as though he realized he hadn't got too much longer to live—he was in bad shape.

Sammy Penn and Joe James made a terrific rhythm section; they didn't need anyone else. All in all, the session turned out very well.

By now, I realized that I'd have to start my own record company; it was the only way to get my recordings distributed. I had been involved with a few projects in England, and I'd learned that you could press ninety-nine copies of a recording before it became liable for purchase tax, which was over twenty-seven percent. If you sold them at two pounds each, it still didn't cover the recording costs.

I thought people would welcome them with open arms, but ten years later I still had some of the original issue of ninety-nine pressings left. I realized that there was only a handful of people who realized what I was trying to do with my MONO label (the name stood for Music of New Orleans). But that handful was fiercely loyal—many of them bought everything I put out.

I'd never heard the E. Gibson Brass Band, and I was determined to record them, but I didn't have any more budget on this trip. There was no one called E. Gibson. Alphonse Spears, the tenor player, ran the band. Cal Blunt, the trombone player, led the band. They were a very tight-knit unit; they would pray together before they started playing at rehearsal, thanking the Lord for their music.

Over the river, I'd been to a cornerstone laying with the Young Tuxedo band. I remember they had Worthia Thomas on trombone, Harold Dejan on alto, and the best drum section in town: Alfred Williams and Emile Knox. You could follow those two all day and never get tired.

The leader was John Casimir on E-flat clarinet. You could hear him wailing over the band from ten blocks away. If somebody was seriously sick, he would knock at their door and ask if they'd given any thought to hiring a band for the funeral. If John came calling, you knew you only had a few days to go. I don't know how he knew, but he did. He used to play with a kind of up and down motion. You could tell where the beat was, just from watching the clarinet. There were people who couldn't stand his playing. Percy Humphrey called him a squealer.

By now, Bill Russell was looking at me as a kind of junior partner. I had asked Alfred Williams if he would consider selling me his snare drum, which had belonged to the legendary old-time drummer Ernest "Ninesse" Trepagnier and dated back to at least 1912. Alfred refused at first, but then he relented, and on the last day of my trip, brought the drum to Bill Russell's store and offered it to me for thirty-five dollars. I didn't have any money, but Bill made a phone call to Al Rose, and he lent me enough to buy the drum.

Dick Allen had put me and Bill Russell down to be extras in a movie that Julia Films were making, called *The World of Night No. 2*. We went to 500 Bourbon, and they were featuring T. T. Red, a big burlesque star. They put us in the front row, and she sat astride Bill's bald head as part of her routine. I've never seen him turn so red. We kidded him about it for years! Still, he needed the money too.

Another film company wanted to film a band down at the docks. They hired Willie Humphrey on clarinet, [Waldren] "Frog" Joseph on trombone, John "Picket" Brunious on trumpet, Manuel Sayles on banjo, Paul Barbarin on bass drum, and Lester "Blackie" Santiago on snare drum. They had to wear plaid shirts and play sitting on cotton bales. Emanuel Sayles took me down there, and we went to get "Picket." He had this little boy with him—it was his son Wendell. He asked if I could look after the kid, who was about six years old. I was paid as an extra; it paid about five dollars.

The way it turned out, the movie people weren't satisfied. The musicians were all busy next day, so they had to carry on until dusk. Picket's wife, Nazimova, came to pick Wendell up. People round here called her "Chinee"—they couldn't manage Nazimova.

Round about then, someone told me that the George Lewis band were playing a private convention job on a boat two hundred yards away. So I sneaked along the catwalk and went on the boat. There was Percy Humphrey, Jim Robinson, Drag, and Cié. I listened to them for about half an hour, sneaked back along the catwalk to the dock, and collected my five dollars from the film company. So I'm probably the only man alive who got paid to listen to George Lewis.

I also managed to make a little money playing my first professional job in New Orleans, on Mardi Gras Day. The band was Kid Sheik, Harold, Albert Warner, Sayles, Slow Drag, and me. It paid about ten dollars, and it was on the top of what is now Maison Bourbon. The job lasted about ten hours, but it wasn't long enough for me.

My money had almost gone, and I had no idea how I was going to get home. It was Harold Dejan who came to the rescue. He said to me, "Look, how would it be if I got you a half-worker, half-passenger berth on Lykes lines?" It was direct from New Orleans to Southampton, and it would save around two hundred dollars against the regular fare, which meant I could stay a bit longer. I remember I had to get a seaman's card. Harold took me down to the merchant marine to get it.

I got a card to say I was a seaman in the U.S. merchant marine. I had to do a bit of "cabin-boying." Strictly speaking, it was illegal. I had to pay a small amount, about a hundred dollars.

I had to meet the SS *Shirley Lykes*. I said good-bye to all my friends and got on the boat down by the French Quarter. There was a small group of what the captain called "guests." Two Dutch boys, an English lady and her daughter, me, and the lady in Cabin 9 (no one saw her the whole voyage). The captain got us together and told us, "I have some bad news for you. The bosun's mate is sick, so we won't be sailing until tomorrow." So I went to Bill's store and told him, "Man, I couldn't stay away from here, so I came straight back." We sailed the following day.

I had to run meals to people in their cabins, the guests, the captain, the bosun, and the ship's carpenter. I never met the crew. I had a little cabin to myself, which was great. The cargo was pig iron. We sailed up the coast and put into the naval base at Norfolk, Virginia. Then we sailed north into the Arctic Sea and saw some icebergs. It was a slow boat. I was at sea about three and a half weeks. The carpenter didn't seem to be doing much; every time I took his food, he would be hand-carving a little totem pole. Over the course of time, we got quite friendly. He was a nice old boy, looked like Burl Ives.

There was a lady in Cabin 9, but she never came out. I would leave her meals outside the door, knock, and go away. An hour later, the plates would be there for me to collect outside the door.

We hit bad weather in the North Atlantic. I wasn't sick, but I was scared shitless. I asked the carpenter, "Do you think the boat's going to capsize?" He told me, "This is nothing. It ain't worth a noseful of snot. You've got salt water on these fries. Get them covered in future!"

When we got in to Rotterdam, the radio started to pick up the BBC from England. The first thing we heard was Kenny Ball's Jazz Band playing "Samantha." Someone said, "Change the station, that sounds awful." They switched to four different stations, and they were all playing the same kind of stuff. It was the beginning of the trad boom.

I left the boat in Southampton, and that was the end of my career in the U.S. mercantile marine.

Back in England I found that Pete Dyer had taken over my English band and had registered the name Kid Martyn Ragtime Band. They had got a drummer with whom they were happy, and they didn't need me back. I went to hear them and they had Cuff Billett on trumpet and Bill Greenow on clarinet. I spoke to Cuff in the intermission, he was really interested in the things I'd found in New Orleans. As a trumpet player, I thought he showed a lot of promise.

Having promise is a weird thing. Keith Smith once needed a replacement clarinet player for his band. Someone said to him, "You should get so-and-so. He's got a lot of promise." Keith said, "Promise? I want something for my money *now*!"

By then I had met my friend Richard Knowles. He used to ride around on a little red scooter, and he always wore a beige corduroy coat and a crash helmet.

My band had established itself as the alternative to Ken Colyer. The main difference was he and his following had established him as a kind of high priest or prophet for New Orleans jazz in England. Even before I went to New Orleans, I wasn't convinced. His music didn't sound much like the records I heard. Everything they played was four beat, and it didn't sound right. It didn't mean much to me.

When I came back from New Orleans, I had a better idea of what I was trying to do. Unfortunately I no longer had a band to do it. I wanted to go back to New Orleans, but my roots were in England, my mother and father and Carole, who I was going to marry; she'd waited eleven months for me.

I called Sammy Rimington, who had been closest to me in my old band. He told me to come to his job with Ken Colyer that night. I traveled in the band bus with them, and Sammy and I talked nonstop about New Orleans. The previous band I had heard was George Lewis with Percy Humphrey, so the Colyer band sounded a bit bland by comparison.

The trad boom was going full blast in England, and there was an unbelievable amount of work for bands. Whatever band I could get together, I knew it would find work. The local fire department would hire one night, the Young Conservatives the night after that, then the church, then the Young Socialists. Bands would split up, and each member would form their own band. Then those bands would split up and the process would happen again. There was no end to it. They had bands dressing up in all kinds of outlandish costume. I've seen them in powdered wigs and frock coats.

The music all had that English beat. To my ears it was the worst music ever, after rap and hip hop. A few days after I came back, my girlfriend

Carole suggested we should go and hear a band called Preacher Hood and his Jazz Missionaries. My friend Gerry Green was playing with them. A gang of us, including Richard Knowles, went over there; it was in a pub called the Star and Garter. I was introduced to the trumpet-playing leader, Dennis Jones. He used to appear wearing a dark gray suit with a clerical collar—Preacher Hood was like his stage persona. I thought he really was a clergyman—he spoke like one.

I was getting acclimatized to this trad nonsense, because it was all over the radio and TV. You saw people playing the most outrageous tunes— "Peter and the Wolf," "Teddy Bear's Picnic," stuff like that. Compared to that, Preacher Hood sounded like a breath of fresh air. They were playing classic 1920s material, and there were a lot of my friends in the band. I went to hear them several times, and then Dennis asked me to join them. I brought in some of the repertoire from the A. J. Piron Orchestra. I lent them some recordings and sheet music. I was with them for several months. I enjoyed it, and it saved the trouble of forming and running my own band.

Then it came time to go back to New Orleans. Richard Knowles and I had become close friends, and he was interested in the same music as I was. We raised the money for the trip by working for Simmon's Brewery, in Staines. If we'd known what was involved, we'd never have gone. We were draymen; we traveled on the beer truck. When you made a delivery, they would send you down in the cellar, and you stood at the bottom of a chute. You wore a special hat with a protective flap and a pad that fitted on your shoulder. They dropped the beer barrels on your shoulder—man, it really hurt!

1962–1965

So the two of us caught the boat together in late January. We had our own cabin. I remember we saw the second James Bond film, *From Russia with Love*, on the boat. We made friends with the drummer in the ship's orchestra, a man called Dai Evans. We were kidding around, and I said to him, "One of these days, I'll be leading a whole New Orleans band. We'll play at your wedding." Years later, I was playing in the Lederhalle in Stuttgart, Germany, with the Legends of Jazz, and who the hell came in my dressing room in the intermission but Dai Evans! He reminded me of what I'd said on the boat in 1962.

We got to New York, checked into a flophouse hotel, and went that night to see Wild Bill Davison. We called on Zutty and Marge. They'd never heard an upper-crust accent like Richard's. I had to translate for them. Then it was back on the Greyhound bus for the forty-hour journey to New Orleans. This time there were no incidents.

When we got to New Orleans, Richard was very keen to see Peter Bocage, whom he called "The Missing Link," which I guess he was, in a way.

I was keen to record John Handy[25]—I'd heard him play alto sax on records. I was eating in Buster's (a musicians' hangout and diner), and Kid Howard came in and said hello. I didn't recognize him, he'd put on so much weight. I arranged to go to Howard's house to talk business. He was living with his mother, who was known as "Small Black," and she cooked us fried chicken.

I told Howard I wanted to record him. At that time, he had only made one record under his own name. After that, he always called me "Boss Man." It really aggravated me—I didn't like it. He was the most peculiar one of all the New Orleans musicians. At the end of a dance, he would take the band's money and hide. Wendell Eugene told me that when he and his brother Homer had a removal business, Howard got them to move a load of furniture for a white man he knew. They never got paid. It was all that kind of thing.

When I found the 1937 recording of Kid Howard playing with Frank Murray, I promised to pay him fifty dollars when I issued the recordings, and he signed a paper agreeing to this. After that, he asked me for the money on a monthly basis. I finally made a copy of our agreement, and mailed it to him. Face to face, he was always very friendly. He was the only real strange one I came across.

I made him leader, so he would get double money, and told him I wanted to get John Handy on alto sax, but I couldn't afford a trombone player. He said, "Don't worry about that. Me and Handy will do whatever you want." I said, "No, do whatever you want; I'll just pay the bill." I wanted to get Joe Watkins on drums. Howard suggested George Guesnon on banjo, which pleased me greatly, and he also suggested Louis James on bass.

John Handy lived out in Pass Christian, about twenty miles out of the city. We arranged to meet together with him at Guesnon's house, and George pretty well chaired the meeting. There was a knock on the door, and there stood this little black man. I've never seen anyone such a dark black. He had little pointed ears that stuck up like the Devil's horns. He never opened his mouth for the first twenty minutes while George held the floor, talking about what they would record and so forth. Then Handy said, "Forget all that. Howard's the leader, let him pick the songs. You hush up now, we've heard enough of your claptrap." After that, George just kept quiet.

Howard wanted to do "Old-Time Religion" but said we could do it as an extra, because it would be very short. I suggested "Should I Reveal" with Handy on clarinet and a second take with him on alto sax.

We recorded at Preservation Hall, which had opened by then. Bill Russell was the recording engineer, and I think Richard Knowles paid for Louis James to be there. When we came to record Peter Bocage, Richard paid for the whole session. Over the years, I've been unjustly given the credit for a lot of things like that. But I did release the Bocage session on MONO records.

Albert Warner, Kid Sheik, and Louis Gallaud came to the Howard sessions; Sidney Montague was the union official. I smoked cigars, and so did Howard and Sheik. So it was kind of foggy in there.

They started off with "Should I?" and I knew I'd hit pay dirt, artistically. Handy had recorded once before, for Ken Mills, but the records had never been issued. Richard made a film of the session on eight millimeter. "Old-Time Religion" lasted a minute and Howard ended it and said to the union man, "I'm not happy with that, Sidney. You can hear for yourself, it's a load of crap." Sidney Montague said, "Alright, Howard, we'll forget that one exists." But he didn't make us wipe it off the tape.

It was the most commercially successful recording I did. Then I spoke to Peter Bocage with Richard Knowles. Richard did a lot of the talking, but he didn't know Pete, and Pete had trouble understanding Richard's accent. Pete was his own man; you couldn't tell him what to do. We had decided to use Louis Cottrell on the session. The only suggestion I remember making (and it was only a suggestion) was that Cottrell play tenor sax on one number. Pete said, "That boy's more suited to the clarinet." We asked him to see how things went on the day. Pete chose Homer Eugene on trombone, Sayles on guitar, August Lanoix on bass, Joe Robichaux, and Alfred Williams. His choices were great, but they were *his* choices. Peter had a quiet authority. He never raised his voice. We asked him if he would play the violin, and he said, "We'll see." That ended that discussion, but luckily, he did. Also, luckily, Cottrell played tenor.

When the session started, Emanuel Sayles was playing electric guitar. Bocage said, "Sayles! Turn that amplifier off. It's too noisy!" That's why there's electric guitar on "Sentimental Journey." It was the first number they did. Apart from that, Pete was very happy with that rhythm section.

Then they did a medley, modulating from "Sweetheart of Sigma Chi" into "Let Me Call You Sweetheart." Pete told Joe Robichaux how to make the modulation, and it sounded great. But Pete wasn't happy, and they made five takes. Cottrell was representing the union as well as playing his clarinet, and he said, "Say, Pete, you know the union rules say we're only allowed three takes." Pete replied, "Louis, please don't tell me about union rules. I'm interested in getting this right, and you're distracting me. I'll do a hundred takes, if that's what it takes." Cottrell said, "Well, alright, but let's try and get it straight." Pete said, "What do you think I'm doing?"

One time we were at his house on Vallette Street, and he reached into this trunk and showed us some music written by Manuel Perez for the Excelsior band in about 1910. Then he pulled out music for a song he'd written with Armand Piron. I was wondering what else could possibly be in the trunk, and he went and got a trombone and played "When the Saints Go Marching In."

He was a complete professional; there was no bullshit about the man. He regarded music strictly as a job. He had heard Buddy Bolden many times. I asked him, "Was Bolden loud?" Pete laughed and said, "That was his biggest asset." He talked about Manuel Perez and Joe Oliver like you and I would talk about next-door neighbors—it was incredible.

He loved Eugene's trombone playing and Joe Robichaux's piano playing. He thought they were the best available in the city at that time.

I don't think he thought of himself as a jazz musician. He'd been more or less forced into that role. He was one of the oldest professional musicians in New Orleans. He answered all our questions about the past out of politeness, but he really wasn't interested in the past.

He could be very critical. He was working with the Eureka Brass Band at that time, and they'd hired Kid Thomas on one job, to substitute for Percy Humphrey. Pete said, "My, what a disaster. That boy really wasn't up to it." But all the New Orleans musicians really respected and looked up to him.

The way the Olympia Brass Band session happened was this:

I offered to record the band, to get it started. I suggested to Harold that he use Anderson Minor; he'd never been recorded, and was quite a force in brass band music at the time, plus Harold was going to use some of the guys out of his band anyway. I know that Harold suggested Louis Cottrell on clarinet, and I think I suggested Albert Warner. Oddly enough, it was Harold that suggested Louis Nelson. Most people would have thought that because I knew Nelson it would have been the other way around. I suggested Cié Frazier; Booker T. Glass was playing with Minor. I suggested Kid Sheik, Harold suggested Ernie Cagnolatti. Actually Harold and I both suggested Sheik, because they worked together in dance bands and all that. I think Jesse Charles was chosen because Harold and I agreed he hadn't been recorded and would be good on the recording. I think that covers everybody in the band.

I said to Harold, "I'm here for six weeks, and I've got a couple of other recordings to do. Why don't you be thinking of a name for the band?" As far as I recollect, he said, "I already know. I'm going to call it the Olympia Band, after Arnold Dupass."

I had a friend in New Orleans called Anthony Parkhouse—he came from Montreal, Canada. I said to Harold, "If you get hold of a bass drum somewhere, I'll get Anthony Parkhouse to paint the name—he's an artist." So Ant (we called him that) painted the bass drum. Harold told him what to put on it: 288-7409 and the Olympia Brass Band of New Orleans, LA, and he did all that, for Harold, at no charge. There was a photographer friend of Anthony Parkhouse called Rudy Haas. He took publicity photographs for Harold. They all liked Harold's million-dollar personality, and they didn't charge him anything; they just wanted to help him. That was how the band got started. So when we made the recording, it was great as far as brass bands went, because it was a band that had come from almost nothing.

I don't think they rehearsed at all. We did the session in Preservation Hall; I've got a movie picture of it. Because I had no funds, at those times, I could only do four numbers, as per the union rules. Actually, with a brass band, I was lucky to do that. The scale was horrendous, and Louis Cottrell being the president of the musicians' union Local 496; we couldn't do more than we were allowed to do, because he was sitting there. Harold said, "The old-time bands used to feature the drummers here; let's feature them"—and that was "Lord, Lord, Lord." They did a funeral hymn, "What a Friend We Have in Jesus," and I remember Harold saying, "Goddammit, you'll never get any feeling in this. Let's just stand and sway to the music." He got the whole band swaying to the tune, especially Harold—he got a real swing, you know? They sat down to play, and stood up for the last chorus. I remember Bill Russell was there, and he didn't think too much of it; he didn't like "modern" brass bands. But he said under the circumstances it was about the best you could get.[26]

I mentioned that Preservation Hall had opened by then. Ken Mills and Barbara Reid started the thing—there's no doubt about that. But they weren't running it as a business; it was more of an artistic venture. Then Allen Jaffe came to town and got a job at D. H. Holmes. I saw him once riding a delivery bicycle, with a basket on the front.

He didn't know anything about New Orleans music when he first came here, but he liked it, and he learned as he earned. I remember him coming into Bill's store when I was there, and asked us how we thought certain combinations of musicians would work. Kid Howard and Jim Robinson had had some kind of misunderstanding with George Lewis, and they didn't want to work for him. It was some kind of humbug. Some years later, I saw the minutes of meeting for Local 496. The George Lewis band had taken George to the union for not taking long enough intermissions at the El Morocco. Brother [Percy] Humphrey had said, "I love the band and I love George, but he's supposed to take a fifteen-minute intermission. Sometimes he calls the band back after ten." George was given a warning.

Jim and Howard were like fric and frac, they didn't want to work with each other. Alton Purnell told me that when they were on the road together, they would buy whiskey, a fifth between them. When they went to bed, they would mark the level of whiskey in the bottle. They each carried a glass cutter for the purpose.

When the George Lewis band went up to New Hampshire, Jim and Howard wouldn't work under George's name, so they had to call the band the Emanuel Sayles All Stars.

Anyway, back to Preservation Hall. The owner, Larry Borenstein, was a businessman. But he was also a kind man; he was very nice to me. By him being in the art gallery trade, he could see a way that art could be a business as well. I guess he saw in Allen Jaffe someone who could run the hall for him.

In those days, you couldn't find a bad band there. The Emanuel Sayles All Stars (George Lewis band) played there two nights a week. Jaffe would hire musicians who hadn't been playing in a long while. If you hired certain men, they came with their own established bands. For instance, if you wanted John Casimir on clarinet, he would come with Andy Anderson on trumpet, Bill Matthews on trombone, Wilbert Tillman on bass horn, Alfred Williams on drums, and Louis Gallaud on piano. My favorite band was on a Tuesday night. Business was slow, but they had Billie and De De Pierce on piano and cornet, Albert Warner on trombone, and Cié on drums. They played the most bizarre material. I heard them play "Daisy, Daisy" and "The Hot Canary."

The audiences then were much the same as they are now. Tourists from Rattlesnake, Indiana, who don't know anything at all about the music.

The last time I went to Preservation Hall, they had an English trumpet player, a saxophone player from France, a banjo player from Nebraska, a piano player from Delaware, and Worthia Thomas on trombone. I asked myself, "What are they trying to preserve?" But I wouldn't criticize them. At least they provide work for musicians, and that must be a good thing.

A lot of musicians have come here from outside New Orleans, and they bring their own styles with them. The sensible ones hire black musicians to play with, but you couldn't do that back in 1962, because of segregation. Lyndon Johnson didn't sign the Civil Rights Bill until 1964. Some of the black musicians call this group of outsiders the English Mafia, although they've come here from all over Europe. Except for when I was in England, I've always worked with black bands, and it's those musicians I've learned from. I was the only ofay in the "1000 Years of Jazz" show, and that was thirteen pieces.

There's a lot of musicians around town now that play for purely economic reasons, and that's not a bad thing. It's simpler that way. Take the average jazz-oriented white player: they might have an unbelievable knowledge of jazz, or in some cases, even an understanding of it. But the average black musician doesn't know anything about that, and doesn't care. I remember years later, working with Wendell Brunious at the Gazebo on Decatur Street. He said to me, "That number you just announced by Montana Taylor. Was he a black guy or a white guy?" He really didn't know. But he could play the number great.

For a long while, the white people all said, "There's no young black musicians coming up. The music will die with this generation." And then, when there were young black musicians coming up, like Wendell Brunious, Leroy Jones, Gregg Stafford, all they did was criticize them.

Some musicians come here and think they're going to change the music, but the only thing that changes music is the audience. You have to play for the people, and you'll never be disappointed. That's always been a thing about this music—it welcomes people in. It's a force, a continuum, it's kept going.

In March 1962, it was time for Richard Knowles and I to go back to England. The trad boom was still going strong, and I had to set about forming my own band; I called it the Camelia band. The trad bands were desperately trying to establish an identity. The music was all the same, so they dressed in outlandish uniforms. We dressed normally, but we were getting plenty of work.

Came the day when my ex-band, which was still working under my name, called to say, "You're getting more work than we are. We'd like you to come back and play drums with us." I thought about it, and decided to go back with them. The first thing I did was to make the clarinet player switch to alto. The personnel stayed the same for the next six years.

When I left New Orleans in 1962, I had told Kid Sheik that I would find some way of bringing him to England to tour with my band.

My friend Mike Hazeldine and I got together and formed the Promotional Society for New Orleans Music. Sheik seemed like a natural person to bring. It was like slicing off a piece of the Ninth Ward and dumping it in front of audiences. He was all for it and said he'd love to come.

We made a record and put the proceeds towards financing the tour. It featured Cuff Billett, Sammy Rimington, Graham Paterson, and me. We bought the ticket for Sheik's travel. Walter Eysselinck, who had done a lot of photography in New Orleans, knew Sheik well. He lived in upstate New York, and he asked us if Sheik could break his journey to spend a few days with them.

Sheik had to get a passport, but had trouble getting his birth certificate to support his application. I don't think they kept black people's records very well in those days. Dick Allen had to take him to the church and get the preacher to swear that he was born when he said, or some such foolishness. When they finally found his baptismal certificate in 1963, he found, at the age of fifty-four, that he'd been spelling his surname wrong all his life. It was actually "Cola," not "Colar" like it appears in a lot of the books.

We didn't know anything about getting him a work permit. I was so naïve, I had got him a one way ticket. Sheik hadn't traveled outside New Orleans much. When you got on the boat in those days, they gave you two luggage tickets. One said "Stateroom" and the other said "Hold." He labeled all his luggage "Hold," so they took it all away and left him in the clothes he stood up in for the duration of a five-day voyage. He wrote me a letter, saying, "Dear Kid, I am on the boat, and they done took all my stuff away. I just have the clothes to stand up in and my trumpet. But I'm having a wonderful time." He posted it on the boat. But Sheik thought that by sending me a postcard, I could do something to ease his predicament.

Richard Knowles went to Liverpool to meet Sheik off the boat, but when he got there, immigration wouldn't let him in the country because he had a one-way ticket and he told them that he was going to play music.

Richard called me and told me the situation. I got the telephone number of Henry Brook, who was home secretary at that time. Somehow I got through to the man himself, and explained that Sheik was a folk artist, that he was only going to play a few little parties with us, and that it was no big deal. Brook asked me, "But why are you doing it?" I said to him, "Haven't you ever bought a friend a beer?" He said it was alright, subject to a few restrictions.

He arrived in May of 1963. We met him with a brass band, and he got out his horn and played with us. I remember it took a lot of persuasion to get Ken Colyer to come and play with the reception band. I never figured out why. We went to Euston railway station in London and met Sheik. About two hundred people turned up.

Sheik got off the train. There was a big banner saying "Welcome Kid Sheik," a brass band and a welcome crowd. He couldn't believe that it was all for him, and he burst into tears; he was a very emotional man.

After the music had finished, we all went over the road to the pub. Sheik was a little reticent, and asked me if they would allow coloreds in there. I said to him, "Man, let me tell you how it is. If you don't want to go in that place, you can choose any other place you want. And all these two hundred people will come with you to that place, and they'll all sit and drink until you want to leave, and then they'll leave too. In this country, you go wherever you want to go." Sheik slowly realized how things were for black people in England. Watching him arrive at the realization was very moving—heartbreaking, really. If we got on a bus, Sheik would automatically go to the back and all that nonsense.

It was the first time a New Orleans musician had been accessible to the public. The George Lewis and Kid Ory bands had visited England, but they always performed in a concert situation. They were packaged and handled; access to the musicians was strictly limited. But here was a real live character, and people could just go up and talk to him for half an hour or more. Not only that, he was very happy if they did. He'd regale them with stories of old New Orleans.

He stayed at my house, and he and my father got to be extremely good friends. A few times he got up at four o'clock in the morning so they could go up to Brentford Market together. All the time, my father called him "Boy," but then my father called everybody "Boy." Sheik knew it wasn't the same as being called "Boy" in Louisiana.

To top the whole tour off, Sheik recorded with my band. We recorded at Egham Cricket Club, with Sammy Rimington, Jack Wedell on trombone, Paul Sealey on banjo, and Barry Richardson on bass. To me, it was Sheik's best record. One night, Sheik, Carole, and I went to the movies—by now, Sheik had got used to being able to sit with the rest of us. We had gone there without knowing what was showing. When the main feature came on, it was *Porgy and Bess,* with an all black cast. It broke Sheik up. He said, "Man, the movie house may not be segregated, but the picture is."

When he left, we drove him down to Southampton to catch the boat. When we got back home, Carole and I sat on the bed and cried and held each other. It was like part of our lives had gone.

I planned to go back to New Orleans in 1963. The trumpet player Cuff Billett wanted to come with me. I thought this was a great idea, because the more of us that absorbed the music, the more we would know what we were doing.

At the same time, I had married my then girlfriend, Carole Martyn, and I wanted to take her to New Orleans for our honeymoon. The night of the wedding, we went down to Southampton and got on the *Queen Mary*. Carole got seasick on the voyage, so it kind of put a blight on the honeymoon. So I mooched about the boat for five days. When we were clearing customs at New York, one of the suitcases fell open and spilled about two hundred condoms on the floor. The customs man looked at me and said, "I see you're on honeymoon!"

Then it was on the Greyhound bus. When we got to New Orleans, we rented a room above Dixieland Hall. You had to go through the hall, up the stairs, and round two sides of a gallery on the second floor.

I took her to Preservation Hall to hear Billie and De De. They had Andrew Morgan[27] on tenor, Eddie Dawson on bass, and Albert Jiles on drums. She got upset watching De De, because he was blind and sick. If anything, the music had improved in 1963 because the musicians had been working together regularly at Preservation Hall. They hadn't yet formed any touring unit. They'd cut away the less commercial bands, like the quartets and Peter Bocage. They also didn't employ the more commercial bands, like Papa French, Alvin Alcorn and Albert Walters.

They'd hit a kind of formula, kind of middle of the road as far as general acceptability. Bands like Papa French worked Dixieland Hall. There was good music to be heard on a nightly basis.

Louis Barbarin played drums with the French band, and you'll meet people who say he was ten times better than his brother Paul. Not for me. Paul was fabulous, a really nice man; it's a shame he died so early. He had this fabulous down-home beat. Having said that, I enjoyed both of them.

Al Clark, who ran Dixieland Hall, had a competitive spirit. But Jaffe had hit pay dirt with the "authenticity" thing. I had a friend who once stayed in one of Jaffe's apartments. He thought he'd do him a favor and clean the windows at Preservation Hall. Jaffe came by and bawled him out for cleaning the windows—it was a kind of falsified funkiness. But it worked. It doesn't really matter how you present New Orleans musicians, the music's going to come through. You can't do anything to funny up the music.

Years later, I went to see the Preservation Hall touring band at the Lincoln Center in New York City. I got there early. I was sitting in the front row, the place was empty, and in walked Sing Miller, whom I knew. He said, "Look at this, oh boy!" There on the stage was a Boisendorfer grand piano, the best in the world. Sing said, "All my life I've wanted to play this." Jaffe came in and said, "Take that piano away. Bring us an upright!" Sing almost cried. The Boisendorfer was the king of pianos.

Jaffe took the profits, but he also put money back into the product, and it worked.

Dixieland Hall wasn't as successful, but Al Clark used to do unusual things to attract people. Once a month, Lloyd Washington would go there and sing songs he'd made famous with the Ink Spots. Every night they'd feature a trio of top dancers: Skeet, Pete, and Repeat. One of them now works as a grand marshal with brass bands.

One night, Carole and I were laying in bed; it was about 3:00 a.m. There was a commotion outside—some guy banging on the other apartments, hollering for Josie. I went out there and asked the guy what all the noise was about, waking us up at 3:00 a.m. He came up to me and pulled out a Smith & Wesson. My attitude towards him changed quickly. He cocked the pistol about a foot from my nose. I said, "Listen, mister, there's no Josie here. There's just me and my wife. Carole, get out of bed." She said, "I can't. I've got no clothes on." I said, "Never mind that—this guy's holding a gun on me." She stood up, and he apologized and lowered his gun. He said, "That bitch Josie rolled me for two hundred dollars." Then he left. We went to bed and I started shaking. It was delayed shock.

Before I came to New Orleans in November 1963, I had approached Doug Dobell of 77 Records with a view to recording John Handy, of whom Doug had never heard. I played him the record I had made with Handy and Howard in 1962. He said, "Well, I don't think much of his clarinet playing, but if you can get him to stick to the alto, I'll put up the money. Who else would you use?" I said Jim Robinson on trombone and Slow Drag on bass. That pleased him; he'd heard of them. I knew it would do Handy a lot of good: Doug had the distribution that I didn't. I decided to use Kid Sheik on trumpet. I just wanted a straight lead; the idea was to feature Handy.

I'd realized that there were a hell of a lot of non-union musicians that nobody had heard of that deserved to be recorded. I had approached

Louis Cottrell the previous year, and he had put his job on the line (he was president of the union) by giving me permission to record enough non-union sessions to make three long-playing records—that is, not exactly permission, but he promised to turn a blind eye. I wanted to re-create the Mighty Four for a recording session. This had been a working band that had enjoyed a long residency at the Melody Inn until the early fifties. The original personnel was still available: Harold Dejan on alto sax, George Guesnon on banjo, Lionel Ferbos on trumpet, and Alec Bigard, drums. At that time, no one had recorded Lionel Ferbos. The only problem was I had no money to pay for the session.

I worked out a solution with the band and approached Louis Cottrell again. Basically, the proposition was that the musicians would defer their fee. Cottrell would hold the master tapes until I could send him the money, and he would then release the tapes to me and pay the guys for the session. I was asking him to act as a kind of stakeholder.

He said, "Damn! You keep coming here asking me for all these things!" On the other hand, he loved to play tenor sax, and I had been one of the only people who recorded him on that instrument. So he knew I was in his corner; he was a great player, and if he had only lived long enough, I would have brought him over to Europe. Anyway, he agreed; if he'd said no, the Mighty Four would never have been recorded.

To raise the money for the non-union sessions, I had written a letter to all my MONO customers back in England. I told them that there would be three albums if they could buy them in advance at two pounds each. I got a very good response, enough to fund those sessions. I was doing everything on a shoestring.

Back in England in 1960, Graham Russell and I had gone up to Manchester to a blues package show featuring Sonny Terry, Brownie McGee, and T-Bone Walker. While we were up there, I had first met my friend Mike Hazeldine. I knew he was serious about New Orleans music. He asked if I would do a recording session for him if he raised the money. Like a lot of other things, I was the catalyst. We discussed things at length and decided to record De De Pierce and a band under his own name, which had never been done before. I suggested Israel Gorman because he hadn't recorded much.

So I was set up to record three non-union sessions—the John Handy session, the Mighty Four, and the De De Pierce session, all in November

1963. I intended to play drums myself on the Handy session. I wanted to get Handy on a prestigious label, and also I wanted to use it to promote my own career. It actually worked out cheaper if I played the drums because in those days, as probably today, the leader got double. So by me being the leader and not taking any money, I was able to record the other five musicians—Kid Sheik, John Handy, Jim Robinson, George Guesnon, and Slow Drag—on the very limited budget I had to work with. If I'd have put myself on drums on all of the MONO records, I would have saved a whole lot of money, but this would have defeated the whole purpose of what I was trying to do, by watering down the music.

Anyway, segregation was still in full force, so we had to be very discreet. Someone suggested that we do the recording across the river in Algiers, in Hopes Hall. It was an old dance hall that had seen better days. If we had done it in New Orleans and the police had got wind of it, we'd have all gone to jail. Even over there we had to keep the shutters closed.

John Handy had invited Carole and I to go out and see him at his home in Pass Christian. We went out there on a Friday by Greyhound bus. It was only a little town, and only about six people got off the bus, including us. There was a police car hanging around the bus depot to see who was getting off. This was the days when civil rights activists were coming in from the North, and I guess we must have looked like a pair of Yankee carpetbaggers or something.

When we got to Handy's house on Third Street, the police arrived as we were knocking on the door. I think the neighbors had called them. The cops asked us what we were doing there, and I said we were just visiting, They turned us back, told us we had no business bothering these people. I knew better than to argue. The police had guns and billysticks, and they'd have parted your hair in a minute. We had to catch the bus back to New Orleans—we couldn't do anything else.

We did manage another visit, and this one passed off without any trouble; it was really nice. The difference was this time a friend of Dick Allen took us there in his car, so the police didn't see us at the bus depot.

Handy had been a janitor at Tulane. When we went in the backyard, there was a one-legged chicken with a crooked neck. Dick said, "Handy! I know that chicken. There can't be two like that." Handy didn't exactly blush, but he looked sheepish and said, "Oh shit! You got me now. I stole that chicken from Tulane." I don't know what they were doing with chickens at Tulane. Maybe the students were studying them.

For the non-union sessions, I wanted to record the Gibson Brass Band, John Henry McNeal and his band, and a band we put together called Cal Blunt's Brown Buddies, featuring the trumpet player John Wimberley.

I recorded the brass band in Cal Blunt's backyard, uptown on Washington Avenue. They always had the biggest repertoire, after the Eureka band. Back then, they were the only band playing "Jesus on the Mainline." Today, all the brass bands are playing it. They did "Shanty Town," "Little Rascal," which is an amalgam of two or three Sousa marches; they had all kinds of stuff. The drum section, Dave Bailey and George Sterling, had been working together for about forty years. Dave Bailey was a funny old boy; you couldn't understand a word he said. He had been Chris Kelly's drummer in the twenties.

The next recording was John Henry McNeal's band, which we did at the Harmony Inn. That for me was the best of the non-union sessions. Because they were non-union, I could pay them below union scale. It was the only way I could afford to do it. They wanted to record to become better known. McNeal's trombone player, Buster Moore, was as good as anybody round here. He had two styles, like Louis Nelson. He could play very sweet or rough, whatever was required.

Then Cuff Billett came into town with a couple of friends. I introduced him to George Guesnon, and they took a liking to each other. Cuff would go round to George's house regularly, and they would play music together.

I recorded Emile Barnes, Eddie Richardson, Sammy Hopkins, and Dave Bailey at Tulane. That wasn't too successful because Milé and Richardson got into a fight. One of them criticized the other's playing. Richardson said to Barnes, "Milé, don't be fussing me like an old woman. You should be wearing a dress." It wasn't the sort of thing to say to Milé, who pulled out a knife and shouted, "Dress? I'll show you all about a dress!" Richardson backed off, and I had to calm them down. I'll never forget it.

The next project was Sylvester Handy's band, with Walter "Blue" Robertson on trumpet and Henry "Dog" Franklin on clarinet, who had been Emile's teacher.

The last session was the Cal Blunt band, which I had looked forward to the least because there wasn't a bass player. Leroy Robinet, the saxophone player, had inherited the orchestrations from Sidney Desvigne's orchestra and later led a band playing those arrangements. He was a good tenor player. I called Cal Blunt the night before the session, and he said, "Man, I'm glad you called. The man I hired for the recording got sick, but I hired this other guy, Frank Murray, on guitar."

Earlier, Kid Howard had told us about making some recordings in the 1930s. He even named one the songs—"Chinatown"—and one of the musicians, Chester Zardis, the bass player. We searched for any trace of these records but couldn't find any. Then who should turn up at the Cal Blunt session but Kid Sheik and Howard, drunk as skunks. Sheik sat in a chair six feet away from the band and fell asleep. Howard said, "Hey, Barry! There's Frank Murray. He's the one who made those recordings with me in the thirties." Frank confirmed this and said they'd been made at the San Colombo club. He still had the recordings, under his bed at home. If the original guitarist hadn't got sick and Howard hadn't turned up by chance, we'd never have known.

At that time Billie and De De Pierce were living in a funny little place that seemed more like a doghouse almost, made of cinder blocks in someone's backyard. They didn't have anything. Billie was tough, used to sing the Dozens and all kind of filthy songs, barrelhouse as hell, but she was a lovely person with a big heart. The pair of them had come up playing for the sailors in dives on Decatur Street.

I remember working with the pair of them once, and De De was complaining that his feet were really hurting him; he thought he had got gout. I told him, "Gout's a rich man's disease; you ain't got gout unless you got a lot of secret money stashed away." He laughed—he loved to laugh. I said, "Let me take a look at this gout." Billie had put his shoes on the wrong feet!

Another time, Billie broke her ankle and she couldn't look after De De, who was of course blind. So they had to send for Billie's sister Sadie to look after them. But Sadie got so drunk that she fell in a fishpond. So they had to send for their other sister, Ida, to travel all the way from Pensacola, Florida, to look after them.

On the recording I suggested that Billie and Twat Butler should sing something together, and that turned out to be "Billie and Twat's Humbug." De De came up with "Smoke Gets in Your Eyes." Then he suggested "Tie Me to Your Apron Strings." It was a great session. I really enjoyed it. Mike Hazeldine had put up the money for it, and we had both wanted to do it.

Then came the time for the Mighty Four session, which was the first recording for Lionel Ferbos on trumpet. I suggested we concentrated on Dixieland material, to bring out the jazz content, since the band had originally played a lot of "straight" and popular songs. They were to play the blues in three different keys, and I remember Lionel had to write out three different lots of music, one for each key. It was like a crutch for him.

Harold insisted that we make the recording at the Melody Inn, which was where they had had their original residency, so we went over there to arrange it. The name had changed to the Wagon Wheel. There was a big white guy standing outside with his arms folded. We had to park about a block away, and he watched us walking towards him as he stood in the doorway. Harold went straight to him and said, "Look! Let me tell you what we're going to do. We're going to come in here and make a recording. This boy here's got a big record company in England. You don't have to do nothing, just get us a few beers and some po'boys. We're going to put your place on the map. We'll put a picture on the record of you standing outside your place. It's gonna go all over Europe—in fact, all over the world!"

The guy thanked us, and we set it up. When the session took place, Cuff Billett came with his two friends and Dick Allen, Anthony Parkhouse, and some people off the street. I still think it was Harold's best session—he plays his ass off. Sidney Montague came from the union to do the timekeeping. When the session was finished, Cuff asked if they could play another number because it was going so well. I explained the union regulations, and Cuff offered to pay the extra money.

It must have been in 1963 that I joined the AFM, the musicians' union. People have made a big deal about it, but it really wasn't. The white local was 174, and the black local was 496. I didn't have to think of it for long. In the black local, I knew the president, the vice president, the secretary, the treasurer, most of the officials, and around 60 percent of the membership. In the white local, I only knew a handful. I asked Louis Cottrell if I could join 496 so that I could make the John Handy recording. He was a bit taken aback, but he couldn't see any reason why I shouldn't, unless it was because I came from a foreign country. The union building was at Columbus and Claiborne, and union meetings were all kinds of kicks.

I didn't see what all the fuss was about then, and I don't see it now, but I'm quoted in books as being the first white American to join a black local. The day I joined, I got a call from *Ebony* magazine. They told me what a wonderful thing I'd done, advancing the cause of freedom, and would I give them an interview or some quotes they could use. I explained that my reasons hadn't been politically motivated, it was just because I knew all the people in 496. They were a bit disappointed, but I didn't do the interview.

I should explain that we didn't have a phone in the apartment; it was downstairs in Dixieland Hall. Someone had to come up from there and knock on your door. I was called to the phone, and a voice said, "This is the Klan. We understand you joined the nigger local today. If you ain't out of it by tomorrow morning, we're going to come and visit you tomorrow night, raise your voice a couple of octaves." I was pissed off, coming down all those stairs to listen to this crap, and I was young and foolhardy. I said, "Listen: let me tell you something. You know where I live, over Dixieland Hall on Bourbon? Be careful when you come up the stairs—there's no light, and I wouldn't want you to hurt yourselves tripping over your robes. I'm in the last apartment on that gallery. It's real narrow—you'll have to come in single file. I'll be sitting waiting in the dark with my shotgun and a box of shells; I'll blast you motherfuckers one by one. Come and see me." They never showed up.

When I went to the union to join up, they said a little prayer first, then they recited the constitution. August Lanoix swore me in.

At the end of the 1963 trip to New Orleans, Carole and I went by Greyhound bus up to Montreal and stayed a while with my friend Anthony Parkhouse and his wife Claudia. We flew back to England from Montreal. We had a cheap deal whereby you caught the boat out and the plane back.

Back in England, Stuart McMillan, a commercial artist who was on the board of *Eureka* magazine, wanted to record the Kid Thomas band, whose piano player, Joe James, had recently died. [McMillan] put up the money for the session. I hadn't planned to go to New Orleans in 1964, because I had just got married, so I had other commitments. Like a lot of other people (Mike Hazeldine was one), Stuart had the money, but he didn't have the connections to make it happen. Dick Allen set the thing up; they used Sing Miller on piano. He didn't last long, he didn't get on with the band. I issued two ten inch albums of Kid Thomas on MONO. One was the Stuart McMillan session, which came out great, and the other one I acquired from Sam Charters.

Dick Allen booked Kohlman's Tavern for the recording. Stuart had asked for the band to play "Blueberry Hill" because he was curious as to how Kid Thomas would play it. Thomas picked the rest of the songs. He chose a number called "Je Vous Aime." Tulane sent a lady called Betty Rankin to make notes, and she mailed me these very specific notes to the UK. She mentioned that Thomas called "Je Vous Aime." Emanuel Paul claimed that it meant "You and Me." The notes also mentioned that a black cat called Thaddeus had appeared at the session. Still, it didn't bring bad luck, and the music came out fine.

Stuart donated the session to MONO records; he didn't ask for any payment. A lot of people over the years have helped me in that kind of way, and I've sometimes got credit that I don't deserve. I guess I was a catalyst for a lot of well-intentioned supporters.

I wanted to bring Kid Thomas and Emanuel Paul to tour with my band because the Kid Sheik tour had gone so well the previous year. Emanuel Paul was completely different from Thomas. Emanuel Paul was easygoing and friendly. Because of the debacle with getting Sheik into the country, I had to get work permits. The English musicians' union would only allow American musicians to work if there was a reciprocal exchange. When Louis Armstrong's band played in England, Freddy Randall's band had to do an exchange tour in the States.

By now, I was running a kind of semilegal racket selling cigars. We bought cigars, cigarettes, and liquor from the American PX and sold them in Brentford Market for a huge profit. In fact, I had two American cars then. One was a black Mercury Montclair, for driving at night, and a white Buick Century for daytime use. People thought I was loaded. That's how I became a cigar smoker.

I arranged the exchange with a guy in Connecticut called Bill Bissonette. I fixed up that Sammy Rimington and I would play in Connecticut with a local band as the exchange for Kid Thomas and Emanuel Paul.

One of my many customers for the cigar racket was the big promoter Harold Pendleton. I mentioned to him in conversation that I was bringing over two New Orleans musicians. I wasn't looking for any favors, but he offered to help me with press reception. He had a publicist, and he introduced me to the guy. They organized a press reception, and helped me with publicity free of charge.

The first concert, on Harold's advice, was set for St. Pancras Town Hall. It was a big venue, but he was confident that we would fill it. Thomas and Emanuel Paul flew into Manchester airport, and Mike Hazeldine and I went to meet them. Thomas got off the plane wearing a tuxedo—he was really eccentric. We booked them into a fabulous hotel in Manchester. The two of them went to bed, and Mike and I went to the bar for a drink. I looked out of the window, and there was Thomas in the hotel garden, rummaging around in the bushes, still wearing the tuxedo. I went outside and asked him what he was doing. He said, "Man, I'm looking for a club. Hey, look, this is perfect," and he picked up a lump of wood. I asked him what he needed it for, and he said, "In case anybody breaks into the room." This was a five-star hotel! But that's just how he was.

The press reception was in London the following day, and the banjo player, John Coles, got completely drunk. He passed out in the men's room, and we had to sober him for the concert that night.

We opened with "Hindustan," and after the first couple of choruses, Thomas turned his back to the audience and rummaged around in his bag looking for a set of maracas—he wasn't exactly Mr. Show Business. But he played like hell. I remember he chided us for playing our numbers too fast. I asked him which numbers, and he said, "All of them."

Sheik had fit in with us, but we had to fit in with Thomas. Emanuel Paul was the eternal diplomat; he agreed with everybody. It was a good tour—we all had a great time.

They were both peculiar houseguests. Emanuel would stay up and drink all night. He was homesick; he would write to his wife every other day. He snored so loud I had to put him at the far end of the house. I don't think Thomas wrote home once. I called his wife, Maggie, on the phone once as a surprise for both of them. I remember him saying to her, "Everything's fine. Tell them boys not to throw stones at my Chevy." That was the whole conversation.

Whatever you cooked for him, it didn't suit. My wife, who was pregnant with Emile, cooked something for him once, and he said, "Tastes like oysters." But because of his accent, she thought he said "Tastes like horse shit." She stormed out of the kitchen saying, "Cook your own damn food!" Most New Orleans musicians can cook, at least a bit, but I don't think Thomas could. At least I never saw him cook.

There was always trouble with him and food, wherever you went. In later years, we were eating together at an airport. The waitress came and said, "Can I help you?" Thomas said, "Yeah. I'd like to see the chicken that lays them two-dollar eggs."

I remember they kept their sweaters on all the time; all the New Orleans musicians felt the cold in England. They stayed about four weeks and went home in June 1964.

In the fall of 1964, Keith Smith called me to say he was bringing over the New Orleans piano player Alton Purnell.[28] He asked me to help him fix the first concert at St. Pancras Town Hall, which I was glad to do. I remember Alton came on stage in a white tuxedo jacket and black hat. My band opened the show, then Alton played with Keith's band. I used to go to Keith's house every day to talk to Alton, and we became good friends. I didn't know that it would benefit me in later years.

At the end of the tour, Keith suggested that he and I form a band with Alton and do a tour of Belgium, helped by a lifelong friend and fellow enthusiast, Rudy Balliu. Alton was a really nice, friendly guy, but he was murder when he was drinking. One night he leapt up on the bar in this Belgian club and shouted, "When Purnell drinks, everybody drinks." He bought about forty people in there a drink. The next day I had to get him to do a radio show. He was badly hung over but he made it, under duress. Then he flew home from Belgium.

The only other major event in 1964 was the birth of my son Emile.

Nineteen sixty-five came on, and that was the year we did a tour with Harold Dejan. The trad boom had ended, but we kept going; we had plenty of work.

All the band loved Harold—how could you not? There was a lot of socializing involved. Harold wanted to see the sights, Windsor Castle and all that. We played all jazz clubs, and made a brass band record with Harold.

At the time, I had a number two band to play straight dances, which at that time was beyond the capabilities of my regular band. We played waltzes, "Mexican Hat Dance," "Hokey Pokey," that sort of thing. My friend Tom Stagg got us a job at a works social for the number two band, and I used Harold. That was really his bag.

At the end of the tour, Harold said, "I wish I could see Paris while I'm here." We didn't have any money—the tour had lost money. But we decided to dip into our savings and we went to Paris for two days. I think he flew home from there. When we were in Paris, he knew of all the places. He wanted to see the Moulin Rouge, the Louvre, all of those places. It was kicks for us, just hanging out with him.

A friend of mine called Reginald Hall had been to New Orleans and recorded the Louis James string band, which I issued on MONO.

Walter Eysselinck, who had taken Kid Sheik to Binghamton, New York, in 1963, had by now moved to England and was working at the University of Sussex. He called me and said, "I understand you're friendly with the folk singer Bob Davenport." I knew Bob well; he was a very well-known performer on the English folk club scene. Walter wanted to hire Bob and I, representing folk music in two different idioms, to perform for the student body.

I had explained that Bob had sung a few numbers with my band in the past, but we didn't have much of a repertoire in common. Walter said, "I don't want any music, just the two of you." The money was good, so both of us went down there for a week. It was the weirdest gig ever; all we had to do was wander around and act naturally, and the students followed us around and took notes.

We got up next morning and went to the cafeteria, and there about eight students were taking notes. I never saw what they wrote. Came the end of the week, Walter was delighted; he thought it had been a great success. He paid us off, and we went home. I still don't know what it was about.

It was in February 1965 that Mike Hazeldine called me to go up to meet the board of Manchester Sports Guild, who were John Pye, Jack Swinnerton, and L. C. Jenkins. They were a successful jazz venue, and they'd brought over several American jazz artists, including Albert Nicholas[29] and Henry "Red" Allen. After the meeting had been going for a while, they told me that they wanted my band to appear there with George Lewis.

We went to Belgium to appear on TV with George—Rudy Balliu oversaw the whole thing. The next day, we started an English tour with George at St. Pancras Town Hall in London. Two performances, both completely sold out.

George was ailing a bit, and the organizers worked out a schedule where he worked one day and took two days off. He was great to work with, but he was hard on me. He was hard on all drummers—Joe Watkins had told me that. He didn't want any woodblocks; you had to play with open cymbal. But I didn't mind. A few years earlier, I had been a little kid listening to him from the peanut gallery, so playing with him was a fabulous experience for me. He led the band—he was very good at it. He wasn't what you'd call a stage personality, didn't say much on stage, except once. We were playing at the town hall in Bath, and he walked to the microphone and said to the audience, "I know what you're thinking: Ain't he cute?"

He was always immaculately dressed, and he once advised me, "Barry! Always keep your band looking smart; dress like that, and you look like you don't need the job."

We made a recording with George for Doug Dobell at a pub in London during a power strike. All of us were freezing, and George wore a pair of lace gloves which he'd borrowed from his manager, Dorothy Tait. I remember him warming up by playing "The Blue Danube." It was wonderful, but the recording engineer hadn't bothered to record it because it wasn't jazz.

The tour lasted about three weeks and made a modest profit for Manchester Sports Guild.

1966–1972

Nineteen sixty-six was a big year for me. By then Harold Pendleton was helping me a lot with arranging tours; he had a lot of connections. He had some kind of roster to smooth out the exchange regulations. He helped the Manchester Sports Guild to arrange an English tour for Kid Sheik and John Handy with my band, starting in March. The people already knew

Sheik from his 1963 tour. It was Handy's first tour, but he was the greatest undiscovered talent. He'd turned down offers to join Fats Waller and Jimmie Lunceford—he preferred his little house in Pass Christian.

For some reason, he was a very troubled man. He talked in his sleep. One time when he was staying with us, I heard him screaming about "She done this to me, she shouldn't have. . . ." I got Sheik and we both went in his room. Handy was standing on the bed, jumping around, screaming, and sound asleep. We had to put the light on and wake him up. But he was the most exciting and swinging musician to accompany—he played with such passion.

Sheik's simple trumpet style left plenty of space for Handy to fill, and they got along really well. Handy told me Sheik even split his leader's fee with him back in New Orleans.

One time at Preservation Hall, Handy went into a blues. There were a group of around four black women in the audience, and they went into ecstasy, writhing on the floor. Handy had them, like a Baptist preacher wailing. He just took them and wrung them out. White people appreciated him as a swinging player, but he took the black message to the black audience.

They stayed at our house, and my father was reading in the newspaper about Concorde. He said to Handy, "John! It says here they've got a plane that can fly from London to New York in three hours." Handy said, "That's eight hundred and nineteen point four miles an hour." I thought he was reading it from a newspaper, but he'd calculated it in his head. He was a surprising man. He wasn't concerned with jazz history, but he'd made it. If he hadn't died so early, he would have enjoyed the same status as George Lewis.

We recorded about eight times with Handy in about a week. We had to make the sessions after the live jobs, making records for George Buck and Doug Dobell. We used all different instrumental combinations. At the same time I was touring with John Handy, Keith Smith was touring a band called the New Orleans All Stars. He had Alvin Alcorn on trumpet, Darnell Howard on clarinet, Jimmy Archey on trombone, Alton Purnell on piano, George "Pops" Foster on bass, and Cié Frazier on drums.

It was the ideal opportunity to record a brass band, and we made a session for George Buck under the name of the Eagle Brass Band. We used Alvin and Cié, Sheik and Handy, Frank Booker, Mike Pointon, Roy Maskell, me, and Keith Smith. It wasn't that successful in my opinion because it had too much solo playing.

In 1966 they hired my English band to play the Knokke Jazz Festival in Belgium, playing in the casino with Albert Nicholas. We rehearsed with Nick, to prepare for a TV show later that day.

We were discussing something or other with Nick, and we heard this god-awful racket. Then the door burst open, and a huge black guy reeled into the room shouting, "Bird lives!" It was Ben Webster.[30] Charlie Parker's widow, Chan, was with him. He jumped on to the stage, grabbed Nick in an embrace, and bounced him up and down.

The broadcast started at 6:00 p.m. We did our part, and then it was time for Ben Webster. You could see at a glance that he was completely loaded. First of all, he demanded some stairs to get on the stage, which was about two feet high. So they rushed around and upturned a couple of wooden boxes for him. Then they introduced Ray Nance[31] on trumpet and violin. Ben took his solo and then put his saxophone down on an imaginary stand that wasn't actually there. His horn crashed on the floor. He said, "Fuck it!" and slowly bent down, picked it up, and put it on the grand piano on the strings, which made the piano sound like a comic musical effect. Then he stepped back onto Ray's violin and smashed it to kindling. This was live TV. They pulled the show off the air.

The booking agent had accommodated my band in a dormitory room, with us all in the same room. In the middle of the night, Ben started hammering on the door, hollering, "I want my money!" He finally went away, and I went after him. I ran him to earth in the men's room. "Man," he said. "I need my money. I did *my* part."

Round about September 1966 I brought trombonist Louis Nelson to England to tour with my band. When I had first met him in New Orleans, he had collapsed in front of me. He was drinking heavily in those days, and he looked terrible. He'd go in a bar, sit and drink until he fell off the barstool, and they'd call his wife to come and get him. He never caused any trouble and he didn't drink all the time; he was able to hold down his job with the Kid Thomas band.

He quit drinking in 1963. He just did it cold turkey—he was a very decisive man. As a result George Lewis took him to Japan, and he never caused any trouble.

After he'd been in England for two days, Nelson was interviewed by the critic Max Jones for *Melody Maker* magazine. It was good publicity for the tour. Max said to him, "Tell me, Mr. Nelson, how long have you been playing jazz trombone?" And Nelson told him, "Two years!" Max Jones said, "Surely you must mean forty-two years?" And Nelson said, "I mean two years. Before that, I was playing music! That was before I joined George Lewis."

The women loved him; he was tall, good looking, very dignified, carried himself well. He had a little scar on his face. He loved women too.

He was a good houseguest, very easy to get along with. Once, Carole and I had gone up to London with him on a shopping expedition. He really appreciated nice things. My wife was admiring a fur coat in one of the windows. Nelson took her in the shop and got her to try it on. Then he said, "Keep it on. It's cold out there," and bought it for her.

Of all the New Orleans musicians who toured with my band, Nelson fit in best. He was just simpatico—he could have fit in with anybody. He was a man of very few words; he'd never have made it as a talk show host. I didn't have that many jobs for him that first time because no one had heard of him.

During the tour, three Italian guys showed up at several of the jobs. One was Guido Cairo, one called Gigi Caviccoli, and one called Carlo Besta. They asked if it would be possible to take Nelson to Italy. They came to dinner at my house and asked if they could call Milan to fix it up. I picked up the phone, and the voice at the other end sounded like mafioso. It turned out to be Luciano Invernizzi, who is still one of my best friends today. Luciano asked if he could take my band with Louis Nelson as soon as the English tour was over.

So we flew to Milan, and Tom Stagg, who was working as band manager, collected everyone's passports during the flight. When we arrived in Milan, he couldn't find the passports—he'd left them on the plane!

We mostly played concert halls, which was amazing, because the Italian tour had been arranged at such short notice. It was the first time I had been to Italy, and I loved the food, the people, everything about the place. Luciano was very hospitable towards us. He loved New Orleans music as much as I did. Whoever I brought over next, he wanted to book them in Italy.

We formed an association, the two of us and Rudy Balliu, called New Orleans Presentations, Inc., which helped to defray the costs of the tours, expenses, air tickets, that kind of thing. So from them on, things got very much easier for me. Two-thirds easier, in fact.

Nelson went home at the end of 1966, and I went back to New Orleans. I wanted to record with Percy Humphrey and Chester Zardis. I played drums, on a set I had borrowed from Sammy Penn. I had to repair the snare drum—it was all messed up. I did another session with Kid Sheik and Earl Humphrey and one with Kid Thomas and Paul Barnes on alto. Those recordings took most of the time on that trip.

The recording with Kid Thomas and Paul Barnes was a quartet session. I drove to pick Thomas up at four o'clock and found him round the back of the house in his overalls, up a ladder painting the house. I said, "Tom, what the hell are you doing up there? We're supposed to be doing a recording session." He said, "Shit, yeah, you're right—I forgot!" He went in the house, came straight out with his trumpet, and made the session—still in his paint-covered overalls. Talk about a functional man.

In 1967 my band was getting very popular. The trouble was, half of them had day jobs and didn't want to play music full time. The other half of the band, including me, wanted to rely on music for a living. So the band just about broke up, which was a shame. I carried on with Dan Pawson on trumpet. The first job we played was at Great Fosters Hotel, which had formerly been one of the stately homes of England. Dan turned up in a tuxedo, which was good, but he was also wearing bright yellow suspenders, a cap on his head, and carrying a plastic gallon jar labeled "hooch"! Luckily, I caught him in the car park and got him to leave the cap and the jar and do up his jacket.

Dan played a little violin with the band, just a couple of numbers. We were doing a job up north when a promoter said to us, "That trumpet player. He plays fiddle, doesn't he? Let him play." Dan danced round him in the dressing room playing "Hey Diddle Diddle."

While he was with the band, they booked us for the Birmingham Jazz Festival with Albert Nicholas. Also on the bill was Ben Webster, which sounded like potential disaster.

Nick was very fastidious, smartly dressed, always wore a little hat. Ben Webster went on before us. He was stone-cold sober, and he played "Danny Boy," "Over the Rainbow," and "The Nearness of You." That's all he played, just three ballads. It was the most beautiful tenor playing I've ever heard in my life. It was entirely the opposite of the previous time I'd seen him.

We went on after Ben and opened with "Buddy Bolden's Blues." Nick was playing, and Richard Simmons, our piano player, said to Dan, "Why don't you play violin behind him? I know he's crazy about violin!" Dan started sawing away, and Albert leaned back and said to Richard, "Tell him to get out of there with that shit!" Dan said to Richard, "What did he say?" And Richard told him, "He wants you to play a little louder, he's really diggin' it."

It didn't work out too well with Dan; he lived in Birmingham and couldn't always make it. So then I formed a band with Keith Smith and Frank Naundorf, a German trombonist who was living in London at the time. Keith was running a record store called "Tony's Turntable." We had an office in the back; we called it ABC Booking. What it amounted to was, if the phone rang in that room, Keith would answer it "ABC Booking." I had a huge blown-up photograph in my house of me with Sheik and Handy playing in Hope's Hall. Keith persuaded me to put the picture on the wall of ABC Booking to give a bit of ambience. Meanwhile, the band wasn't doing too well, mainly because it had two bandleaders. It just didn't work.

I finally said, "Look, Keith, it's not going to work out. I'm just going to take my picture off that wall and call it a day." He shouted, "Don't touch that picture!" He swung a punch at me and I floored him. He grabbed the phone, shouting, "Police! Police!" I told him he had to dial 999 first. I left by the back alley, and that was the end of that. The band had existed for five weeks.

I was floundering a bit at this time; for the first time, I couldn't see a clear path to what I wanted to do. The trad boom was long over, but some nightclub owners or promoters would still sometimes hire a band as part of a variety package. Some guy called me from the Dolce Vita club in Newcastle. He wanted to put us on the bill with Jayne Mansfield, who was touring in England. She was a nice, friendly girl; I remember she sent champagne to our dressing room. But she really wasn't much of a singer—she sang flat all the time. She always opened her act with "Call Me." The audiences liked her, mainly because of the tight dresses she wore. She didn't have a manager; she was handling her own career. Not long after that job, she died in a car accident on U.S. 90, just outside New Orleans.

It was in 1968 that I took a band to America. Durel Black was running the first New Orleans Jazz Festival, and Harold Dejan had persuaded him to book us. I took Teddy Fullick, Sammy Rimington, Pete Dyer, Jon Marks on piano, Brian Turnock on bass, and me. We did several jobs in the U.S. traveling to the festival. In a diner south of the Mason-Dixon Line, we were leaving when the waitress said, "Y'all come back now." Pete Dyer had never heard the expression and he said, "I'm afraid we won't be able to. We have to travel back via Los Angeles. We won't be coming back this way. . . ."

When we got to New Orleans, we were traveling in an old station wagon I had bought from Jimmy McPartland the trumpet player. There was a band playing on the street near Buster's, and the guys were so excited they all jumped out and ran off to listen. I locked up the car and went into Buster's to inquire about cheap accommodation. When I came back, the car had been broken into, and all our suitcases had been stolen, plus the snare drum that Alfred Williams had sold me.

We went to National Shirt on Canal and bought six matching red shirts. We were playing at the Municipal Auditorium the next day—we had to do something. We played some A. J. Piron tunes, like "Kiss Me Sweet" and "Red Man Blues." Pete Dyer was worrying me about what we would play on stage, and I told him I didn't know until we got up there. This was in the wings, and Gerry Mulligan was standing nearby talking to Dave Brubeck. The boys told me later that Pete asked Gerry Mulligan if *he* knew what songs I was going to call.

I stayed at Lars Edegran's place in 1968, and we went over to Peter Bocage's place after his death to try to acquire his collection, which both of us had seen. The guy who answered the door told us, "That collection's worth millions of dollars." We had been thinking in the region of two hundred, so we left. About two years later, we tried again, and the same guy told us, "There's two guys came all the way from Europe to buy this!" He was talking about us. We never did get the collection.

When we returned to England after the U.S. tour, Teddy Fullick got sick and had to quit.

In 1968, Handy made a tour with the band. Sammy Rimington played tenor and clarinet, so we could feature two reeds in duet format on the jobs.

Clive Wilson came in to replace Teddy on trumpet, and Dick Douthwaite joined on clarinet. At that time, he was strongly influenced by Milé Barnes. Frank Naundorf had stayed on trombone, despite the Keith Smith fracas.

In 1969 we did a tour with Andrew Morgan. By now, because of having New Orleans Presentations, Inc., with Rudy and Luciano, we could afford to be more ambitious. "Big" Morgan was a huge, affable man, and both my sons can still remember him crashing up the stairs at home with his big feet.

He lived on Monroe Street in New Orleans, and he had a straight job cleaning lawyers' offices. There was a room at the side of his house that he converted into a little candy store. He'd sell candy to the kids. He was a really nice man, very friendly to young musicians. He'd invited my whole band out to his house in New Orleans. At the time, he was playing with the Young Tuxedo Brass Band.

The Morgan tour was very successful and wound up in March 1969. He had a lot of unusual repertoire.

In the latter part of 1969, we brought Emanuel Sayles to tour in England. He was a revelation. I would never normally hire a banjo player, but he was an exception. He surprised us all—he was a great entertainer. We had learned "Astoria Strut" from his early records, and he played exactly the same solo that he had recorded forty years earlier. Everybody loved him; he'd play anything—it made no difference to him.

Nineteen sixty-nine was also the year my second son, Ben, was born.

In 1970 Alton Purnell came back to England in February to tour with us. He liked to do unusual material, old pop songs like "Lies," "Dardanella," even "The Lambeth Walk." It was another good tour, but largely uneventful.

I was being interviewed once, and the man asked me, "Of all the New Orleans musicians you've toured with, what's the question they ask most frequently?" I told him, "That's simple: 'Is breakfast included?'" That's the truth, and Alton was no exception.

In the spring of 1970, I met the Swedish trombone player Freddie John, who was on his way home from New Orleans. He played a job with my band, and I hired him on the spot. This was a Saturday night, and on the Monday he left with us to go back to the U.S.

The first job we played was the "Hello Louis" concert at the Shrine Auditorium in Los Angeles. Louis [Armstrong] was there—the show was for his seventieth birthday. Alton had got us the job. All the jazz clubs in California had got together to put it on. The last job was in Madison, Wisconsin.

It was in Los Angeles that I first met Floyd Levin. I went to a party at Floyd's house, and there I met Ed Garland, Alton, Barney Bigard, Tyree Glen, Nesuhi Ertegun, Maxim Saury, and Claude Luter, from France.

July Fourth was the night of the concert. The Los Angeles musicians' union, Local 47, wouldn't let my band play on the stage. Don't ask me why. So we had to play in the pit. The management came and said, "Could you play a bit longer? Sarah Vaughan's forgotten her dress." In the end, we played for over an hour, Leonard Feather was in the audience, and he gave us a surprisingly good review; he didn't usually like our kind of music.

At the end of the show, I was standing in the wings, behind one of the scrim curtains. A few yards away, I could see Louis Armstrong waiting to go on. The show had run late; it was eleven forty, and if they ran past ten minutes after twelve, the auditorium would charge a massive premium. I heard Floyd Levin, who was behind me, say to one of the organizers, "We'll have to ask Louis to cut down his act." Louis heard him, too. On stage, Barney Bigard was playing "C Jam Blues." Louis walked on stage to tremendous applause, stopped the band and sang "Hello, Dolly!" Nobody was going to cut his act down.

Earlier I saw Hoagy[32] walking across the stage and said, "Mr. Carmichael, I wonder if you'd mind signing this little book?" He said, "I haven't got the time for that now!" and kept walking. I thought, "Big-time bastard, what would it have taken?"

A little later, there was a knock on my dressing room door. It was Hoagy Carmichael. He said, "Were you the man that wanted that book signed? I'm so sorry, I was busy with stage directions earlier." He sat down, chatted for a while, and signed the book. I changed my opinion of him right away—he was a real gentleman.

My band, which you could call the British contingent, had had to drive across the United States in a beat-up old station wagon under our own steam. Maxim Saury and Claude Luter, who had met Louis when he was filming *Paris Blues*, were sponsored by the French government—first-class air travel, even sent vintage champagne as a birthday present for Louis.

There seemed to be a happy community around Los Angeles, no race problems—it wasn't anything like Dixie. That's why so many New Orleans musicians had moved there. It was just more free and easy; they could just go wherever they wanted.

Before we went back to England, we made a side trip to New Orleans, and I approached Percy Humphrey about making a European tour. He said, "I'd love to do it, but you'll have to talk to the Preservation Hall people." Percy was working a lot for the hall at that time. They gave me the big time but finally agreed, as long as it was a short tour.

We met Percy with a brass band—it was freezing cold. The band met on the top floor of the airport car park, ready to play when Percy came out of the elevator. Within two minutes, three carloads of airport police came and stopped us—it was typical of England.

He taught me a lot about how to play New Orleans music. He was himself a band leader of many years standing, and he was very outspoken. He spoke very slowly, and he'd look at you over his glasses and tell you, "Look, that trombone gotta get underneath there" or whatever it was.

I remember he really enjoyed drinking with Jon Marks; I couldn't keep up with them. He had the same air of quiet authority that Peter Bocage had. They were the same kind of leader. Back in New Orleans, he had hired his brother Earl to play trombone with the Eureka band, on condition he didn't drink. Earl rigged up a plastic straw under his shirt that came out at the collar. He could just stop playing for a couple of bars and take a drink whenever he wanted. Percy watched him like a hawk, but he never caught him.

New Orleans music was built on cornerstones like Percy Humphrey. And when he played over the out-choruses with the Eureka, it was the most glorious sound you'd want to hear.

We had a few jobs scheduled with Percy in Sweden, a country I had never visited before. We went to the venue for what we thought was the first concert of the tour. I remember how cold it was, well below freezing. When we arrived, the place was packed with jazz fans and tables with American flags on them, with a bottle of Jack Daniel's about every six places.

Percy told us, "It's going to be a long night. Better go easy on all that whiskey." I said to the promoter, "You'd better bring us some iced water. We'll take it carefully with Jack Daniel's—we have to work here tonight." He said, "No, you don't have to play here tonight. This is a welcome party for you and the band." I told Percy and we both got as drunk as skunks.

After about two hours, the promoter came and said, "OK, we're ready for you now." I said, "What, to carry us back to the hotel?" He said, "No, to play the concert upstairs." I said to him, "You told me we didn't have to work in here tonight." He said, "Not in *here*—upstairs!"

It was really embarrassing—the band leader and the guest star were completely out of it. I couldn't keep time, I couldn't even see the drums. It wasn't a case of being unprofessional, but we really thought we had a night off. We worked hard to make up for it the next few nights.

One of the tour dates was Uppsala, way in the north of Sweden. We came back from there in three cars. We hit some ice on the road, and the car I was in flipped over on its roof. We were hanging upside down in our seats, and the car started to catch fire. We scrambled out, and Percy and I stood on the road, warming ourselves by the flames. We were feeling alright until one of the Swedish guys said, "Yes, it is alright until the flames die down; then if a car does not come, we will die." Luckily enough, a truck came by with one spare seat. We put Percy in it and gave the driver a few dollars to drop him at our hotel. We carried on throwing wood on the burning car to keep warm. At around five in the morning, just as it was getting light, a car passed and took the rest of us back.

The next night, Percy told the audience all about it and said we would open by playing "Lord, Lord, Lord, you sure been good to me"—especially this morning.

Percy flew back to the States from Stockholm. The band continued to Italy because we had some work booked in Milan. But when we arrived, I got the news that my father had died, so I caught the next flight home to England.

* * *

We did a tour with Don Ewell early in 1971. He didn't like the band, and he made it very obvious. It got to the point where the band didn't like him, although we loved his piano playing. It wasn't a happy tour.

When we went to Denmark, he looked really miserable when he got on stage. The promoter even said, "Can't you get rid of that old man, and bring back Don Ewell?" He thought Jon Marks was Don Ewell.

We had come to Copenhagen from Ireland, and Don had been paid in Irish currency, and it got stolen by the hotel chambermaid. Her boyfriend had put her up to it, but Irish currency is easy to trace in Denmark, and they got caught.

It was around spring 1971 that I decided to give up music as a living. I raised hogs for about six months. I'd had enough of all the hassle of leading a band; I'd lost my motivation. One day, John Defferay, the clarinet player, came out to my little farm. He had been working in his father's business but had decided to quit and earn a living playing music. He wanted me to join him. I told him I couldn't do it, I was too involved in the hog farm. All my money was invested in it, about two thousand pounds. John said he'd lend me the money to get out of the farm; I could pay him back when I could afford it. So I was back in the band-leading business.

We had Jon Marks on piano, Wesley Starr played bass, and the Japanese trumpet player Yoshio Toyama. This all came together at the end of 1971. Early in 1972 the band went back to the United States. I had Geoff Cole on trombone. We played in New Orleans and Los Angeles. One of the jobs we played while we were there, a man came up to me in intermission; he had this great-looking woman with him. He said to her, "This is my good friend Barry Martyn." He was out to impress—I'd never seen him before in my life. But I didn't want to shame him in front of his girl, so I said, "Hey, man, how are you feeling? Good to see you again." He said, "What can I get you to drink?" I told him "bourbon," and he asked me what kind. I said, "Generally speaking, three." He said, "You mean three kinds of bourbon?" I told him, "No, three bourbons." I was drinking in those days. While he was away, I slipped this girl my address and went to lunch with her the next day. Her name was Barbara Westerberg, and she later became my second wife.

Back in England, we did a tour with Alton Purnell and a record. Nelson came in March. After Yoshio left to go back to Japan, I had no trumpet player. Ken Colyer had disbanded his regular band several months earlier. So I had a band and no trumpet and he had a trumpet and no band. Also, we shared the same booking agent. He suggested that we should amalgamate and acted as a go between.

If it was a Ken Colyer job, he would lead the band, and if it was my job, I would lead. The first job was mine, and I told him, "Look, when the front line stands up, it's the last chorus. You end it there." They stood up but he kept going. The band stopped and just looked at him playing on his own. When he ran the job, the tunes seemed to last months. But after we got adjusted we got along together well.

I didn't think he sounded anything like a New Orleans trumpet player, but he did have an original and very personal style. He was a big Bunk Johnson fan. Contrary to what most people think, he was very right-wing, politically; he was dead against trade unions. One of his great heroes was General George S. Patton. I had quite a few things in common with him, but I liked him more as a man than as a musician.

This band only lasted a couple of months. We used a guy called Ken Blakemore on trombone, who was a good, punchy player.

Came November 1972, Carole and I had split up. I left England on November 5 to join Barbara, to whom I had been writing in Los Angeles. When I took off from London airport, my plane was delayed. I was pretty broke, and when I changed my money to American currency, I had thirty-seven dollars and forty cents. But I knew I was going somewhere I could make it.

I knew there were lots of New Orleans musicians in Los Angeles. I knew I could form a band there, and I knew it would be successful. As the plane took off, I saw the fireworks for Guy Fawkes night, all over England. I took it to be a good omen.

Virginia Minstrels, with Barry Martyn's father as Mr. Interlocutor (in top hat)

Clive Blackmore, Barry Martyn, Bob Rae, Gerry Green. England, 1956.

Kid Sheik, John Smith, Harold Dejan

Punch Miller, Kid Thomas, Louis Nelson. New Orleans, 1961.

Kid Thomas band audition for Riverside recordings

Riverside recording. Alfred Williams, Jim Robinson, Ernie Cagnolatti, Louis Cottrell, George Guesnon, Alcide "Slow Drag" Pavageau. New Orleans, 1961.

Sammy Penn

Drum lesson with Cié Frazier. New Orleans, 1961.

Cié Frazier, George Lewis, playing on boat. New Orleans, 1961.

Alfred Williams hands over his snare drum. New Orleans, 1961.

The Emanuel Sayles All Stars—Jim Robinson, Kid Howard, George Lewis, Alcide Pavageau. New Orleans, 1961.

Kid Sheik arriving at train station. England, 1963.

Sammy Rimington, Barry Richardson, Kid Sheik, Barry Martyn,
Jack Wedell, Paul Seeley. England, 1963.

Barry Martyn, Jim Robinson, Kid Sheik, Slow Drag Pavageau, John Handy,
George Guesnon. New Orleans, 1963.

De De Pierce, Barry Martyn, John Handy. New Orleans, 1965.

Emanuel Paul, Barry Martyn, Kid Thomas. England, 1964.

Handbill for George Lewis and the Kid Martyn Ragtime Band concert, 1965

Barry Martyn and Cié Frazier. Eagle Brass Band recording session, England, 1966.

Earl Humphrey, Kid Sheik, Paul Barnes, Barry Martyn, Lars Edegran.

Andrew Morgan

Barry Martyn with Olympia Brass Band. New Orleans, 1968.

Percy Humphrey

Jon Marks, John Defferay, Wesley Starr, Ken Colyer, Barry Martyn, Del Evans.
England, 1972.

Sellout at the Wilshire Ebell. Los Angeles, 1973.

First Legends of Jazz public performance: Louis Nelson, Barry Martyn,
Ed Garland, Andrew Blankeney, Alton Purnell, Joe Darensbourg.
Santa Monica, California, 1973.

New Orleans Society Orchestra. Los Angeles, 1973.

Legends of Jazz with band bus. Los Angeles, 1975.

The Legends of Jazz. Standing: Barry Martyn, Sam Lee, Alton Purnell,
Adolphus Morris. Seated: Louis Nelson, Andrew Blakeney.

Andrew Blakeney

Louis Nelson

Barry Martyn, Louis Nelson. Ohio, 1975.

Adolphus Morris

Joe "Brother Cornbread" Thomas

Cozy Cole, Floyd Levin, Barry Martyn. California, 1976.

Barney Bigard

Benny Carter

Joe Darensbourg, Andrew Blakeney, Dinah Shore, Alton Purnell,
Barry Martyn, Ed Garland. Los Angeles, 1976.

"1000 Years of Jazz" show with dancers Chuck Green, Raymond Kaalund,
Buster Brown, Ralph Brown, and Lon Chaney accompanied
by the Legends of Jazz. New York, 1979.

Clyde Bernhardt

Floyd Turnham

Society Brass Band: Freddy Johnson, Daniel Farrow, Joe Torregano,
Chris Tyle, Barry Martyn. New Orleans, early 1990s.

The Young Men of New Orleans: Ed Frank, McNeal Breaux, Barry Martyn,
Orange Kellin, Wendell Brunious, Freddy Lonzo. Finland, 2002.

Barry Martyn

1973–1984
ACROSS THE STATES AND
AROUND THE WORLD

For decades, California, and particularly Los Angeles, acted as a home from home for New Orleans musicians and the New Orleans population at large. Successive generations were lured west by the prospect of an improved climate, a more relaxed attitude to matters of race, and better employment prospects. Some of the demand for New Orleans music came from the Hollywood studios. In the days of silent movies, directors would hire jazz bands to "pace" the action. After the introduction of sound, they still hired jazz musicians to create a relaxed ambience on the set; pianist Jelly Roll Morton was offered this kind of work in 1940.

Later there was work in the recording and TV studios for such musicians as Dr. John, Earl Palmer, and Harold Battiste. The New Orleans population in south central L.A. was so large that a black Mexican named Rodriguez opened a store selling filé gumbo, hot sausage, and other nostalgic tastes of Louisiana.

In 1919, trombonist and bandleader Edward "Kid" Ory had moved from New Orleans to Los Angeles, where he spent several years leading a band of fellow expatriates. In 1922 Ory's Sunshine Orchestra (which included bass player Ed "Montudie" Garland) made the first ever jazz records by a black band, at a studio in Santa Monica. In an interview with Bill Russell, Ory recalled:

> I planned to go to Chicago, but I thought I'd try Los Angeles first. I got all the boys together to discuss the trip to California. We met at Ben Mulligan's saloon. We had supper and drank a lot of whisky and wine. Louis, Johnny Dodds and Joe Lindsey and myself all got on our knees and swore we were all going to California.
>
> As soon as I got to Los Angeles, some dude called Lee Locking from Galveston, Texas, called me. He was opening a place called the Cadillac on Central Avenue, across the street from the Union Station. He asked me to put a band in there. So, after I'd been there about a month, I wired for my band to come out and sent tickets. I sent a telegram to Manetta, who had been playing piano with us, to get the band together. But by that time Louis had taken the job on the boat, so Manetta got Papa Mutt. The porters at the depot told Johnny Dodds that he'd better not go to California, as he would be sent back, like Frankie Duson, 'cause he couldn't read. He

wouldn't come. So Manetta got Wade Whaley for clarinet. Papa Mutt and Whaley had been working together at the Bungalow with Walter Decou and Mack Lacey. Mutt and Whaley both wanted to go and Whaley was unhappy about working with Decou. Then Joe Lindsey didn't want to go, he wanted to be a gambler, so, as Lacey had just died, Manetta got Alfred Williams from the Sam Morgan band. We didn't take no bass.

When they got to Los Angeles, I hired a furniture wagon and two mules, just like we used to do in New Orleans, and set up the band on the wagon. The houses in California all had galleries on the second floor, but the doors were blocked off and people didn't sit out on the upstairs porch like they did in New Orleans. When the people heard the music they all come busting down the doors on the galleries. That night the Cadillac was packed with people.

In 1921, my band was working at the Creole Café on Third and Wood in Oakland. One day the Spikes brothers asked me to record for them. They were both saxophone players and they had a music store in Los Angeles. So we took the train down from Oakland and made the records in about three hours. That was the first time I had seen a recording set up. They had big horns, like the ones we used to sing into—megaphones. We each played into a different horn, but the drums and things, they'd just shake along. Some of them came out alright. "Ory's Creole Trombone" came out good the first time, but some of the others we had to go over again. That's the time we had Dink Johnson playing with us. We picked him up in Los Angeles, when Wade wanted to stay in Oakland. Dink patted his feet too loud, so we put a pillow under his feet. He was overpowering the drums and everyone else. The drum didn't record properly. Ben Borders was our drummer. He was a fair drummer, but he didn't have much of a beat on the bass drum.

Henry Martin was the best drummer I ever had in my band. Next, Ed Robertson, the boy that started out with me. Might have to pull a straw between the two of them to figure out which one was better. Henry Martin was like a metronome. You couldn't move him after you thumped your feet. You couldn't make him go faster and you couldn't make him go slower. Any number with funny lyrics to it, like animal noises, he would find a way to imitate the noises. He mainly worked in Storyville with Manuel Perez, but he would work for me too when I needed him. Then he quit drums and took up the guitar for a while, but he starved. I heard he went back to drums later, but he couldn't make it. Joe Lindsey was also a very good drummer.

In 1925 I wanted to see the country. Oliver was waiting for me in Chicago, so I disbanded. I had two bands, I gave one to Papa Mutt and the other to Tudi Garland.[33]

Ory returned in 1930, but in 1933 he retired from music to run a chicken farm, also working in a railroad office and as a mail sorter. He reemerged in 1942–43, playing in clubs like Billy Berg's and the Tip-Toe Inn, where he was spotted by Orson Welles. Barney Bigard met him again in Los Angeles in the early 1940s. Interviewed by Barry Martyn, Bigard remembered:

It was right around this time that I met a real old friend. Talk about a "ghost from the past!" Who should I bump into one day but Edward "Kid" Ory. Of course we knew each other from my childhood, when my uncle Emile led Ory's band. The depression had hit Ory hard and he looked a whole lot different. He told me he had been out of the music business for a long while and hadn't played a job in years. Some of his old band were living out here too. Tom "Papa Mutt" Carey, Ed Garland, Bud Scott. All "home-town boys." Ory told me that he had been working as a cook for a while but when I met him again in 1942 he was sweeping out the city morgue for $12 a week. I hated to see the old man in such bad shape so I asked him to bring his horn over to the Capri one night and play a bit with my band. He wasn't too keen at first but I kept after him and finally one night he showed up with his trombone.

Now here's where I want to set the history books straight. I have read a hundred times that Ory joined my band on bass. I don't know where that story came from but ask yourself this. What would I want Ory to play bass for when I had one of the best bass players in the country in the band already? Ory never did play bass with us. He came out there that night with the trombone and that's how it stayed.

So this night he came out and he stumbled through a couple of his old compositions, "Muskrat Ramble" and "Ory's Creole Trombone." When he played the little spot he just broke it up. The people came all around the bandstand to see him. I mean this guy was a museum piece to them. Most people thought he was dead, let alone still able to play his trombone. The guys all asked me what I wanted with that old man but I just told them, "Look. Can you make that audience break up like he does? Don't worry. He'll bring plenty of customers in this place." He did too. We never advertised him being there except for little cards on the tables. That was the only thing bearing his name, but nevertheless he pulled people in every night.

*Ory and I got to be even better friends socially. He would go crawfishing
with me when the season came. He was like an uncle to me through those
months but later on he seemed to change completely. But at this time we
were buddies. He and his brother John were in some kind of partnership.
Ory lived on 33rd and Central and his brother lived on 37th Street. John
had this huge back yard where they were raising chickens and a few turkeys.
I don't know who was the dumber: Ory or the turkeys. When I went out
there first, these stupid turkeys wouldn't eat and so Ory had put some little
chicks in there to show them how to eat. Ory wasn't far behind them. If one
of these turkeys caught a cold here he would come with the big cylindri-
cal thing and shove Vick's Nasal Spray up their nostrils. Getting around
Thanksgiving he would get lots of orders for these birds but there was one
great big one he said he was going to keep for him and his brother. So
come Thanksgiving Day they had sold all the turkeys save for this big one
and when they came to get him, he had died. He swallowed a pebble and
couldn't get it through. They had to go out and buy a turkey to put on the
table. Boy! That was something. They had that business for a good while,
Ory and his brother John, but then the brother took with a heart attack and
died and Ory disposed of the place.*

*Anyway he was working regular with me at the Capri, but then fate took
a hand in both our careers and he was pushed into going for a band of his
own.*

*Orson Welles was in Los Angeles. He had gained world-wide fame for
his two pictures* Citizen Kane *and* The Magnificent Ambersons *and was
now running a series of broadcasts called the "Mercury Theater Broadcasts" over CBS. He was also working on a filming of* Jane Eyre *at the
same time. Apparently Welles had asked Marili Morden of the Jazzman
Record Shop if she could locate a real authentic New Orleans jazz band
for a broadcast in March of 1944. She turned to Ory who put together a
band with Mutt Carey, trumpet, himself, trombone, Buster Wilson, piano,
Bud Scott, guitar, Ed Garland, bass and Zutty Singleton on drums. Zutty
was the only one that was working on a regular job at the time. He was a
"biggie" around Los Angeles. They didn't know who to use on clarinet and
someone suggested Jimmie Noone. He too had a regular job working with
his own quartet at a place called "The Café de Paris" on Hollywood Boulevard. They had the band downstairs I remember.*

Anyhow they made that broadcast in March of 1944 and they were so well liked that the people wrote in and called in to say they ought to put the band on again.

Over the next few years Kid Ory's Creole Jazz Band worked and recorded regularly, appeared in various Hollywood movies, and toured Europe. At various times, the band included Ed Garland, bass; Andrew Blakeney, trumpet; and Barney Bigard or Joe Darensbourg, clarinet. We shall be hearing more about these four men later in the story. Bigard continues:

I went to [Ory's] funeral in 1973. They put him away New Orleans style with a band of music and some of his old buddies played for his last ride: Andrew Blakeney, Teddy Buckner, Norm Bowden, Sam Lee, Alton Purnell. I know they played "Just a Closer Walk with Thee" over him and cut out down the hill with "Muskrat Ramble" and "Ory's Creole Trombone" and that was the end of an era.[34]

Within a few days of my arrival in Los Angeles, Kid Ory died in Hawaii. They shipped his body back to L.A. for burial at Holy Cross cemetery. I went to the funeral; when I went to view his body at the mortuary, Alton Purnell came and introduced me to Andrew Blakeney outside the funeral home. Everybody wore black, white shirts, black ties.

Joe Darensbourg and Ed Garland came; he must have been about eighty-eight years old. He was almost blind, so I led him in to where the coffin was. He leaned forward to within an inch of Ory's face, squinted for a few seconds, and said, "He looks pretty good, don't he?" Then there was a commotion because the funeral procession had to climb a hill to Holy Cross gravesite. They had a brass band with some great musicians called the Resurrection Brass Band. Alton Redd, the bass drummer, couldn't make it up the hill. So they gave me a parade cap and asked me to play bass drum. They had Teddy Buckner and Andrew Blakeney, Mike Delay on trumpets; Joe Darensbourg and Sam Lee on reeds; Dan Barrett, Frank Demond, and Gordon Mitchell, trombones; Sylvester Rice on snare drum; and Art Levin on bass horn.

They asked me not to play on the funeral marches because I wouldn't know the music although I thought, "Shit, they must be going to do some really complicated stuff." Then they opened with "Closer Walk with

Thee." I played along and they were amazed, but I'd been playing it already for over fifteen years.

Up at the graveyard we played some jazz numbers, including Ory's "Muskrat Ramble." The reverend complained about me smoking a cigar in the graveyard.

Alton [Purnell] told me he was playing with an old-style Dixieland band called the New Salutation Tuxedo Jazz Orchestra. So one night I drove him to work, in Fullerton.

They had the job five nights a week. Alton introduced me to the drummer, Teddy Edwards, who was originally from New Orleans. He had been on the road a long time with Joe Liggins before moving to Los Angeles. He was a very quiet guy, but he had a devilish sense of humor.

After I'd been to a few of their jobs, Ron Going, the bandleader, called me and asked me to meet him at Frank Demond's house the following Saturday to discuss business. I was all for it; my thirty-seven dollars had dwindled to around fourteen by then. I went to Frank's house in Huntington Beach, and they offered me the job with the band. I told them I didn't want them to fire Teddy Edwards, because he'd always been friendly towards me, and that I had to get in the union before I could work. Also, I was planning to form my own band, so I'd be unreliable for them. They said, "Well, look, we have to work a job this Saturday in Redlands, and we'd like to use you on that. Teddy will be glad of a night off and the union won't bother us out there."

I picked up Ed "Tudi" Garland to take him to the job. He was a really powerful player, even at his age. The job paid ninety dollars, which made me several times better off.

The next thing I remember was going to a local jazz club. It was very strange. They would have people like Ray Coniff playing with a bunch of lousy musicians. They would have all the professionals mixed with all the amateurs.

Floyd Levin, whom I'd met and who had been very nice to me at the "Hello Louis" concert, was very influential in Californian jazz circles. They described the job as a "jazz bash." Floyd had a table reserved up at the front. Alton and I were invited to sit with him, and he introduced me to Barney Bigard. I remembered Barney as a man of extremely few words. He just sat there, didn't speak at all. He was playing the next set, and he suddenly said, "Do you want to play the next set with me?" We got up there, and while I was changing the drums round, I heard him say, "You on the banjo. We won't be needing you, you can get down. And you on the tuba, if I hear too much from you, you can go too." So I liked him right away.

After about six numbers, we went back to sit at the table. Barney said, "You played good. You don't like banjos? Put it there," and he shook my hand. I knew I'd made a friend. Then he started talking to me—it was as though I'd passed some kind of test. Anyone who doesn't like banjos can't be all bad.

After that, I started to get a band together. I recruited Alton Purnell for the piano chair. Then I went to see Tudi in Watts. All the black musicians lived there except Barney. I asked him to join this band I was forming, and he said, "Who have you got?" It was sort of like the Magnificent Seven. I told him, "So far, I've got Purnell." Tudi said, "Purnell? I'll tell you one thing—black is bad. Who else will you get?" He was light-skinned himself. I said, "Well, I haven't heard anybody out here that plays trombone the way I want, so I was planning to use my friend Louis Nelson from New Orleans." When Nelson arrived, Tudi said to him, "How's my friend Eddie Cherie doing?" Nelson told him, "Eddie Cherie? Shit, he's been dead for forty years!"

I asked him who he'd recommend for the clarinet job, and he advised me to ask Joe [Darensbourg]. And for the trumpet, he thought either Mike Delay, Andrew Blakeney, or Norman Bowden.

I went to see Joe Darensbourg. He had a nice house out in the Valley. He was black but very light-skinned, and he passed for white. He'd married a white woman called Helen; she was a beautiful person. He'd made quite a bit of money from his hit record "Yellow Dog Blues."

We sat outside drinking root beer, and I told him about forming the band. Really, I thought he was probably a bit out of our league. He asked who I had already got, what kind of work I was fixing to do, and if I intended to rehearse. I told him I intended to rehearse the band until it was where I wanted it to be. He said, "That's good. Call me when you're ready." I left there elated. I couldn't believe it.

The trumpet choice was between Mike Delay and Andrew Blakeney. Blake was originally from Quitman, Mississippi. He was around seventy-eight years old. When I asked him to join, he said, "Oh sure, if Joe Darensbourg's going to be there." I fixed a rehearsal for the following week at the union hall, on Hollywood and Vine.

I had become friendly with an old Kansas City blues singer and drummer, Jesse Price, who was a friend of Barney Bigard. He was a barrelhouse sort of character; if you were his friend, he'd cuss you out. If he was polite, it was because he didn't like you. I was telling him about needing to get in the union, and he said, "You come down there with me on Monday, boy." We went to the union building, and the first person we met was Lawrence Brown,[35] the trombone player, who directed us to the president's office. He marched straight in and told the president, Max Herman, "Hey Max, this man's from England, and he needs to get in the union. I know the rules say he should wait six months, but he ain't got that long to wait." Max said, "Well, you know, Jesse, we have certain rules here." Jesse told him, "Don't be talking that shit about the rules! If it hadn't been for all the people I talked into voting for you, you wouldn't be sitting in that chair, you motherfucker. There must be some way you can bend the rules."

The president said to me, "What's your case? Are you going to be putting anyone out of work?" I explained that it was exactly the opposite, and that I'd refused to take a job from Teddy Edwards when it had been offered. Furthermore, I'd be making work for musicians, and I named the people I was fixing to hire. They drew up the papers, and I joined the union right there. So I was ready to work.

A couple of days before the rehearsal Floyd Levin called to invite me and Barbara to join him and his wife, Lucille, at a jazz concert on the Thursday night. After I had sat in with the band to play "Ory's Creole Trombone" (the drummer didn't know it), Floyd and I went out to the foyer to talk business. I told him about my band, and who was in it. My plan was to put the band on in a concert and maybe ask Barney to do a guest spot. Floyd was behind the idea straight away. It was always like that. Everything we did, we did together. Never needed a contract, everything was done on a handshake. We decided that we would work on an equal-shares basis. He said we could use his office downtown. We put up fifty dollars each and called the business Crescent Jazz Productions, after the Crescent City. I think the name was Floyd's idea. It was all decided on the spot.

We asked Barney that same night to headline the concert, and he agreed straightaway. By then, I was seeing him quite a bit socially. He and his wife, Dottie, would come round, and we'd all get drunk. He drank Coors beer by the case, and she drank whatever you had. I once saw her drink a whole bottle of tequila on her own. I was strictly Jack Daniel's myself. When we got pie-eyed, Barney would say, "Let's call Zutty in New York. I know he doesn't go to bed until 4:00 a.m." So we would pass the phone round, telling Zutty jokes and stuff.

Anyway, we started looking for a concert venue. The Shrine Auditorium was too big, so we tried the Wilshire Ebell Theatre. It was perfect for us; it held about eight hundred people. We booked the place, and I called Nelson and told him about it. We printed tickets and bumperstickers, and Floyd and I drove round at night stapling bills to telegraph poles. We never got caught.

Floyd's regular business was called Parvin—he sold barbecue aprons, pot holders, all that kind of stuff. And here he was, respected local businessman, putting up illegal posters in the dark. Next door to the office was a Mexican restaurant on Twelfth and St. Pedro, and we used to eat there. They never seemed to give us a bill, and I asked Floyd if they mailed the bill by arrangement. "Mail me a bill?" he said. "I own the place." He and his wife were beautiful people. They were devoted to each other; they would hold hands like young lovers—it was really reassuring to see.

Meanwhile, we started to rehearse, without the trombone. People would come to listen to the rehearsals. That old style of Dixieland hadn't been heard around Los Angeles since the Kid Ory band. In fact, people used to ask us, "Is this a tribute to Kid Ory?" which it certainly wasn't—the only real problem was getting them out of the Ory way of doing things, because three out of the five of us had been in the Ory band for so long. People like Eddie Miller and Mattie Matlock would come to the rehearsals and sit in with us. We rehearsed every week, and the band began to get a little discouraged because we had no paid work and the Wilshire Ebell job was months away. The other Los Angeles musicians were laughing at us. They called us "the rehearsal band" because we never had a job.

Finally, it came time for the concert. At first, ticket sales had been very slow. Floyd and I had agreed that if we couldn't turn our fifty dollars each into five hundred each fairly quickly, then we might just as well get out of the business. And if we couldn't turn that into five thousand in three months, we were wasting our time.

Leonard Feather called me and asked me over for an interview. Not many people liked him, but he was nothing but nice to me. The interview appeared in the *Los Angeles Times*, with a big picture. The publicity was great, ticket sales picked up, and a week before the concert, we had sold out.

We got the sound engineers to hook up some speakers at the front of the theater, and about thirty people stood out there to listen to us.

We called the Ebell concert "A Night in New Orleans." First we had a made-up band, which I called New Orleans Society Orchestra. It had Mike Delay and Andrew Blakeney on trumpets; Sam Lee and Joe Darensbourg, reeds; Dan Barrett on trombone; and Alton, Tudi, and me. We played some scores of the A. J. Piron band, like "Kiss Me Sweet" and "Purple Rose of Cairo." Then we did a tribute to Kid Ory, which featured Dan Barrett on trombone, who was seventeen at the time.

Lloyd Glenn did a solo piano spot, and then it was time for the Legends of Jazz, featuring Louis Nelson. Barney Bigard and Trummy Young both did a feature with us, and we finished the concert with the Eagle Brass Band. It tore the audience up. They'd never seen a New Orleans brass band before. It was a huge success with great reviews in the papers.

It put us and the band on the map. We made good money, paid the musicians good money, and everybody was satisfied. From there on, we never looked back. Everything we did seemed to have the Midas touch.

We talked an entrepreneur, Milt Larsen, into putting on a concert with the Legends once every three months. He had a place called the Magic Castle and another place called the Santa Monica Playhouse. They also sold right out. We started running New Year's Eve dances with the Legends. That sold out too. The ticket price was twenty-five dollars, including two splits of champagne. I asked Barney to do the first New Year's Eve dance, but he turned me down. He just didn't want to work New Year's Eve, although I told him his fee would be six hundred dollars.

After the Legends had played the first number, Barney appeared on the stage and asked to sit in. He sat there all night and played up to the finale at 1:00 a.m., and we didn't pay him anything. But that's how he was. Maybe he just did it to help us.

I had booked a European tour for the band. It was round about then that the Los Angeles musicians stopped calling us "the rehearsal band."

We did a cross-country tour of the United States, using contacts I had made when touring with my English band. I owe a lot to those people who booked us; men like Arthur Eldridge, Donald Hyde, and Jack Head, who had the Massachusetts Bourbon and Chowder Society; Floyd Wakefield; Al Volmer. Al was an orthodontist, a wonderful guy. He would fix musicians' teeth for free. Punch Miller had his teeth fixed there.

When Al went to a dentists' convention in Chicago, he looked up George Mitchell in the phone book. It was a business address, and when Al got there, George Mitchell was the white vice president of the company. Al apologized for the mistake and explained that the George Mitchell he was looking for was a little black man with a humpback. The vice president said that he'd never heard of this other George Mitchell, and then his secretary said, "Wait a minute. I don't know his name but the guy who parks the cars in the parking lot has a humpback." Incredibly it turned out to be the right George Mitchell, who had played cornet on Jelly Roll Morton's records in 1926!

Al went on to operate the Harlem Jazz and Blues Band with Tommy Benford and Clyde Bernhardt. We always had a party at Al's house at the beginning of a tour. It was in Long Island, New York, and the guest list was amazing. Zutty Singleton was always there, Wild Bill Davison, people like that.

The trombonist, J. C. Higginbotham, had been in hospital, so of course he hadn't been allowed to drink in there. He was coming to one of the parties as soon as he got out, and Al was anxious to keep him sober because he really couldn't play at all when he was drunk. I drove into Harlem to pick him up and took him up to Larchmont. When he got there, he took the trombone out of the case and played brilliantly, just as you'd expect. Unfortunately, someone started slipping him drinks, and after about an hour it was all over.

In later years when Zutty got sick, Nesuhi Ertegun of Atlantic Records would send a chauffeur-driven car for him if he had to go anywhere. I called him to play with my band on a job in Hartford, Connecticut. He said, "Just a minute. I'll look in my book." He came up there in a chauffeur-driven Buick Century. He was old and a bit past his best, but it was beautiful to see him.

The first tour we did in the States with the Legends went east, and Joe Darensbourg hadn't traveled east since 1948. I paid Geoff Bull, the Australian trumpet player, to travel with us, sell records, and be the utility man.

The tour finished with a job just outside Chicago. It had been very successful and put us on the map in the United States. From there we flew direct to England. After a couple of jobs, Joe took sick with influenza, and we had to leave him behind. Local jazz buff Dave Bennett very kindly took him into his house in Basingstoke.

We kept the tour going, and I hired Rudy Balliu to take his place. He was nervous as hell—his hands were shaking. Anyway, he soon settled in and it was fine. Then we went to Scandinavia and finished the tour with Sammy Rimington.

We weren't exactly homesick, but California was such a beautiful state to live in then. At the end of each tour I would shout to Andrew Blakeney, "Hit it, Blake!" He would lead us into "California, Here I Come," and the band would play its heart out. Touring with those guys I was in seventh heaven.

When we flew back into Los Angeles, Floyd and Joe came to meet us in our new band bus, a bright yellow Dodge Sportsman with "The Legends of Jazz" painted on the side. It had power steering, room to stretch out and sleep, and customized wire cages for the instruments and luggage. It was a real pleasure to drive, and we traveled in style.

I conferred with Floyd briefly, and we decided to tell Joe to keep the check we'd given him in advance of the tour, even though he hadn't done most of the jobs. He wasn't normally an emotional kind of guy, more of a nonstop joker, but I remember how touched he was. He had tears in his eyes when he said to me, "Man, nobody ever did anything like that for me before."

Let me tell you a little bit about how the guys in the band were. I'll start with Andrew Blakeney. People would always see us arguing; we'd argue all the time about music. He thought I was a show drummer; I don't know where he got that idea from. He couldn't understand why I would make two beats to the bar on the bass drum, which was the way I had been taught. He was hard on New Orleans musicians—he thought they were all trying to play lead. But the one thing we did have in common was that we were both serious bourbon drinkers. The more we drank, the more argumentative we got.

Once we were on the road, and a tire blew out. Blake came to me later and said, "Look, I know those tires cost more than two hundred dollars.

Here's a hundred dollars." He was that kind of a guy. Everybody liked him. When we went to New York, Lester Boone, the tenor player, who had recorded with Louis Armstrong, would come to see him. And Lionel Hampton was likely to come and see him wherever we were. Blake had given Hampton his start with Les Hite's Orchestra in Los Angeles. He would come to Andrew like a little boy coming to his daddy, and he was one of the biggest stars in the United States.

Blakeney could play just about anything on the trumpet, but he would always put himself down. He would say, "See, I'm really just a copycat." Personally I don't think he copied anyone.

He had a finger missing from his left hand, and when we'd argue he'd point at me with this missing finger. He had a crazy sense of humor. His wife, Ruthie, could drink too. I remember she once invited us over there to eat, and just before dinner, she passed out on the bed. We had to serve ourselves.

Blake, Joe, and Tudi had all been with the Kid Ory band, and they were always telling stories about that band.

Joe used to exaggerate; he had a fund of outrageous stories, and we'd just laugh. But once in a while, his stories would be confirmed, usually by Tudi, who'd also been there. Joe would say to the audience, "I played this number for the King of Belgium, and he presented me with one of those old castles that they have out there—one brick at a time."

He told us that he'd been on a train traveling with the Ory band, going through Brazos Bottom, Texas. The train stopped, and an old peckerwood got on and said, "Well, you boys, I got a field of cotton out there, and I have to get it picked by sundown. I guess you'll help me, won't you?" They said to him, "Man, we're musicians. We didn't come here to pick cotton." But they and the other black people on the train had to get off and pick the man's cotton before they could continue. Tudi confirmed that story—he'd been there.

Joe was born in Ville Platte [Louisiana], and Alphonse Picou had been his teacher. He'd started traveling when he was very young, on the road with Doc Moon's medicine show. They'd sell elixir to people, play a little music first to draw a crowd. He'd lived in Seattle, Washington, for a while.

We stayed in a motel in Cicero, Illinois, once, and it was freezing cold. There was a Chinese restaurant about half a mile away, and that's where we went to eat. Joe said to us, "Watch me bullshit this damn Chinaman.

Hey! Do you know who I am? I used to play clarinet with Louis Armstrong. We used to come in here all the time. I'm the one plays clarinet on 'Hello, Dolly!'" And he sang it for the Chinaman. He told us, "You wait until the end of the week. I'll get us a big discount." I had left a credit card at the place, and we were running a tab.

Every day we ate there, and every day Joe would lay this jive on the Chinaman, complete with "Hello, Dolly!" When the end of the week came round, the man brought the bill, and he'd separated it individually. He said, "All you men, I take 10 percent off your bill. But *you* (meaning Joe), you bullshitter. I add 10 percent." Joe blustered but the man threatened to call the cops, so he had to pay. After that, he stopped telling stories for a while.

We used to showcase Alton Purnell in a piano feature, usually in the second half of the show. I heard Joe tell him one night, "Purnell, you play so well. I swear the audience would rather listen to you than the whole band. I'm going to speak to Barry, see if I can get him to give you two solo numbers." Alton thanked him, and Joe said to me out of the side of his mouth, "Dumb cluck! All we have to do now is keep adding a number a week, and pretty soon, there won't be anything for us to do." Blake and Joe had all these vaudeville routines. The audience loved it.

We used to rehearse a lot, which Louis Nelson hated; he just couldn't see the point. I don't know why he was so lazy. But only about rehearsing—when he got on stage, he would play his ass off. Often I'd get him to play the lead on the trombone. It gave a different flavor to things. He was completely unflappable, a man of few words. He used to look out for Tudi and look after him. But they eventually had a falling out over something, and Nelson said, "Shit! From now on, old man, you look after yourself." And he meant it. When Nelson finished with you, he finished with you.

There's a picture of the Legends band on stage, with Nelson leaning over talking in my ear. A lot of people assume that he's talking about music, but he was actually saying, "Look, fourth row, five seats in. You can see her blue drawers." He loved women and stayed active well into his old age.

Whenever we arrived at a new town, most of the band would get some sleep before the show. But Nelson and I would get dressed up and take a walk down Main Street. He loved nice things, like Gucci shoes and Borsalino hats. We came to a store in some little midwest town. He saw a camel-hair coat in the window, similar to the one I was wearing. He asked me how much I paid for mine. It had been around three hundred dollars, which was expensive in those days. We went in the store, and Nelson said to the sales clerk, "Have you got that beige camel-hair jacket in size forty-four long?" The guy said, "Well, they're quite expensive." And Nelson said, "I didn't ask the price. I asked if you had it in forty-four long!"

We played in some little town in South Dakota and stayed in the only hotel in town, next to the bus depot. I bought a pack of cigars in the depot; the cost was dollar ninety-eight. I gave him two dollars, and he gave me eighteen dollars and two cents change. I said, "Look here, I gave you two dollars." And he said, "We're sick of you city slickers coming here. You must think we're all stupid. I gave you your change—be satisfied. Just stop bothering me." So I left there with a pack of free cigars and a sixteen dollar tip.

Playing in those little towns was easy on us. The furthest distance between them would be a hundred miles, and some were only forty miles apart. The dignitaries usually invited us to a reception, and the guys were always polite and well behaved. Up there in the mid-seventies there wasn't too much racist crap.

But one time we went to a place called Crookston, Minnesota, way up north. We parked in front of the motel, and I went in and told them we had reservations. The desk clerk, who could see the bus and the band through the glass doors, said, "No, you haven't got reservations here." I pulled out the written confirmation, and he snatched it out of my hand and ripped it up. He just came right out with it: "I'm the owner, and I'm not having those damn niggers in here." This was Minnesota in the mid-seventies.

We found a place that would take us, but only if we used the back entrance and stayed in our rooms until it was time for us to go and play. The manager said she didn't want us annoying her guests.

Another time, we played a concert down south, in Cherokee, Arkansas. About nine o'clock the following morning, we all went to a diner for breakfast before we hit the road again.

We were waiting to be seated and the waitress said to us, "Aren't you the guys that played the concert last night? I'm going to bring you to a special room for your breakfasts." We all looked at each other, thinking shit, it's the same old South. Welcome to Dixie. She led us through the restaurant and put us in a back room and left us to get the menus. We all sat there, grumbling about the customs of the South, until she came back. Then she said, "I want to say how much I enjoyed that concert last night. It made me feel so good. I wanted to put you in alone so I could give you really special service, and whatever you want to order, I want you to know it's all on me." As we left, all the diners applauded us. It goes to show, you never can tell.

I only saw Nelson rattled once. I was discussing the next album we were going to make with Floyd. I suggested that we ask Barney to record with us, and Floyd was in complete agreement. That was the sort of working relationship we had—we never really disagreed about anything. I talked it over with Barney, and we decided to use two clarinets so Joe would also be on the record. When we had discussed how the music would be, the only thing left to talk about was Barney's fee. I asked him what he would want, and he said, "Scale." I said it was ridiculous for him to work for just the musicians' union scale, and he said, "If you feel that bad about it, you can pay me the leader's fee and you take the sideman money." It was unheard of. I've heard him turn down RCA Records, all kinds of people.

Anyway, I called Nelson to tell him about the session. I said to him, "Next time you come out, we're going to make a record with Barney Bigard." There was complete silence on the other end of the phone. I said, "Louis, are you there?" He said, "Yeah. I'm here. But shit—*me* make a record with Barney Bigard? Goddamn, if that don't beat all!" He sounded completely stunned, and that's the only time I've known him be overcome in all the years I knew him.

Barney turned up at the session with five little pieces of paper—they must have been about four inches by one inch. It was the intro to a blues called "Legends Boogie." I remember him saying to Tudi, "Don't give me that lazy-ass bass playing. I want four beats to the measure. Purnell! Give me a four-bar introduction to 'I Surrender Dear' in the key of C." Purnell played something and Barney said, "No, no. Wait up. I don't want that." Alton asked, "Was it too fast?" And Barney said, "No, no." Alton asked, "Was I playing too much?" And Barney said, "No, it wasn't that." Alton said, "Well what was it, then?" Barney told him, "Play better!"

We'd parked the band bus outside the studio, which was a stupid thing to do, because we were making a recording without telling the union. Suddenly, in came Lawrence Brown, who was the union recording official. He'd obviously spotted the bus with "Barry Martyn's Legends of Jazz" all over it. He asked us, "What's going on here?" Barney told him, "You can see what's going on—we're making a record. Get out of here, stop worrying us. If you turn me in for this, I'll tell the union about the illegal records we made with Duke." Of course they'd worked together in the Duke Ellington Orchestra for about ten years. Lawrence went away, and we never heard any more about it. We were lucky: if it had been anyone else from the union, we'd have been fined and all kinds of disciplinary crap.

I'd known Purnell for several years, ever since first meeting him in England in the fifties. He was a very volatile man—he'd blow up in a minute. People say that his temper had caused a lot of trouble in the Bunk Johnson band. He was always fine with me—we were friends. But I've seen him blow, lots of times. At the Crescent Jazz Productions office, we had a piano downstairs, and that's where we did all our rehearsing. I've seen Purnell get into a humbug with Blake, leap up from the piano stool, throw his hat on the floor, and jump on it.

He claimed he could read music, but I don't think he could. He could certainly read chord symbols; he knew how the keyboard worked. He was my favorite singer of all time; I've seen him make women in the audience cry, he put so much feeling into it.

He had little tiny hands—he could barely stretch a ninth. He lived on West Seventy-Fifth Street in Watts. He was separated from his wife, although in his later years they got back together. He loved living in Los Angeles.

Ed Garland, Tudi, was the real legend of jazz. You couldn't get any more legendary than that. He was always supportive to what I was trying to do, and very friendly. I went over to his house once, and he said, "Come out to the garage." He could see his way to his own garage, but I would always lead him onto the stage by the hand.

I opened the garage door, and there was this beautiful car, an old green Chrysler. I said to him, "What's this? Are you collecting antiques?" He said, "No, this is my car. I bought it about two months before I went blind. Sit in it." It was spotless and beautiful, a 1958 Chrysler. The mileage stood at 203!

Whenever you went there, he'd give you ice cream and put the ball game on TV. When that was finished, he'd sit and talk about the old days.

He could talk about Buddy Bolden, Manuel Perez. In fact, he had music for "Sally Trombone" in Perez's handwriting. I still have that music today. He'd left his home in New Orleans very early and had been in San Francisco during the earthquake of 1906.

He was always perfectly in tune, and he could do more with a two-bar break than most bass players could with two choruses of solo. He was a little bitty guy, always sharply dressed. When we were up in Banff, Canada, it was freezing cold. Being blind, he didn't bother drawing the curtains, and I could see him through the motel window. He smacked his head on a hanging lamp and punched it back right away. I think he thought there was someone in the room with him. He didn't put up with any shit!

We took a short trip to Minnesota, and we didn't take the bus—it wasn't worth it. We flew into Chicago and drove hire cars from there. We were leaving O'Hare airport, a blizzard came on. We were playing at a ski lodge, and I was in the bar when Nelson came to tell me I was wanted on the telephone. The thing is, he was just wearing a singlet and pants, and it gave those rich customers something to look at. Tudi said, "Damn, that boy ain't got much couth."

On the way to the job, Tudi and Purnell got into an argument about where the old basin had been in New Orleans. Disagreement led to death threats, and they both wanted to get out of the car and fight it out. Tudi was about ninety years old at that time. Ten minutes later, on the stage, it was all forgotten.

He stayed with the band until he got too sick to carry on, which happened in Hanover, Germany. After he came back to Los Angeles, he couldn't play with the band anymore. Time was taking its toll, and Tudi was the first one to go. Percy Gabriel applied for Tudi's job, and he came to do a job with us in Grand Rapids, Michigan. Musically, it worked out OK, but then he told me he wanted twelve hundred dollars a week, which was a hell of a lot in those days. I said to him, "Percy, we got this the wrong way round. How about me joining you?"

When we got back to Los Angeles, we started using Adolphus "Dolf" Morris. His original musical training had been with a Scottish pipe band. His first job was a recording session we did for Capitol Records. They kept it on the market for about two months, and because it didn't sell a million copies straightaway, they withdrew it. Now, you can buy them on the Internet, and they're fetching around five hundred dollars apiece.

Dolf came from playing with Johnny Lucas, and he was a hell of a guy. Johnny came up from playing with Jess Stacy. He was a trumpet player; he was a big fan of New Orleans music, and he'd played with George Lewis's band. He was permanently confined to a wheelchair. If the phone rang at home, he had to crawl across the floor to answer it. He was paralyzed, and he'd had a trumpet made with special long valve stems so that he could play it. He'd had a car modified to suit his disabilities so he could get around. He'd come to my house; I'd carry him up the stairs and set him on a chair and we'd sit all night listening to records and drinking. He was the most amazing man I ever met in jazz.

The next one of the originals to drop out was Louis Nelson. He called me to say he had a problem, he was sick. I asked what the problem was, and he said, "Heart." I asked him was it serious, and he said, "Yeah." He was always a man of few words. So I got Preston Jackson, who'd recorded with Louis Armstrong and Jimmie Noone in the old days. He suited the band fine, replacing Nelson for the tour we had, and Nelson's band jacket fit him.

Nelson came back in the band after the tour, but he had to leave again—we were doing too much touring. I was lucky to get Clyde Bernhardt on trombone.

Joe Darensbourg left, and my first choice for a replacement clarinet was Franz Jackson, but he didn't want the job, so I got Brother Cornbread [Joe Thomas]. They all liked him in the band, but he was a bit goofy. Blake couldn't understand how a man could play so much clarinet and not know what he was doing. He played strictly by ear, didn't know anything at all about music.

He brought a different thing into the band. Less musical, but closer to the old-time New Orleans style. He was a great entertainer. He'd dance "Ballin' the Jack" on the stage. Barney liked him; he called him "Brother Cornball." He would keep his teeth in all the time, and take them out to play. Nelson would keep his teeth out all day and put them in to play. Joe Darensbourg saw this and said, "I can't understand those boys, wasting all that money. They could just get one set between them."

Before Tudi left, we were playing a place called Al Capone's in Sacramento. The way in to the club was through a phone booth: You had to lift the phone, ask for Joe, and a door opened in the back of the booth.

Cornbread had a son called Little Joe, who wasn't little at all—he was built like a tank—and he came there and brought maybe twenty people with him. They had a great time, drank a lot, danced. They were pretty boisterous, sent pitchers of beer over for the band and so forth. Tudi said, "Look at them spooks. They got no business in here. We shouldn't be playing for these coloreds."

Then after Cornbread left, I got Sam Lee in the band. He was a great entertainer, and a good asset.

So by around 1978, the band had changed quite a bit. We had Sam Lee on saxophone, still Andrew Blakeney on trumpet, Clyde Bernhardt on trombone, Adolphus Morris on bass, and Purnell on piano.

The "Night in New Orleans" show had started in 1973 in the Wilshire Ebell, and every year after that we were running an offshoot band called the Louisiana Shakers, which included Alec Burrell and Sammy Rimington.

We started booking the "Night in New Orleans" into Europe and got a ten-day tour. We played at the Berlin Philharmonic, the Deutsches Museum in Munich, the Stadthalle in Vienna. By now we'd made a recording of the Pelican Trio, which was me, Duke Burrell, and Barney Bigard. Milt Larsen booked us at the Santa Monica Playhouse, and it sold right out.

We booked the trio as part of the "Night in New Orleans" show, which that year was featuring Cozy Cole.[36] He had an arrangement he'd worked out. It called for all the house lights to go out, and he would feature with fluorescent drumsticks—it was a hell of an effect. The tune was "Caravan."

The Pelican Trio was closing the first set, and we also had "Caravan" on our play list, so I told Barney we'd have to change it. "No, man, the hell with that," he said. "Let them change." He wouldn't budge. He was so hardheaded.

Another time, we decided to do a tribute to Duke Ellington. We already had Barney Bigard, and the drummer, Louie Bellson, agreed to work for union scale. Ray Nance was very sick, and it was difficult for him to travel. I called him about appearing with us. He was on dialysis. I arranged that we'd meet him with a doctor at the airport, and he had a blood transfusion immediately.

He played "Come Sunday" on the violin. Barney came up to me in the wings and said, "I've never heard anything so beautiful. Don't ask me to follow that. Let's just finish the concert now." After that concert, we went out for a crab legs dinner, and Ray flew back to New York. Three weeks later, he was dead.

In 1976, I went down to Jimmy Ryan's in New York. Max Kaminsky was playing trumpet there, and I asked him if he would consider playing with our package show. He said his fee would be three thousand dollars a week. I said we couldn't pay that much; it was equivalent to half our payroll. He came back with "Can you make it three hundred?" What a reduction!

Then one year, Barney got sick and we had to find a replacement headliner. Floyd and I went to see Benny Carter[37] to ask if he was interested. He was really concerned about Barney, who was his friend. He asked which hospital he was in and asked how his wife was coping. He readily agreed to help us by doing the job, and he just wanted the same money as we would have paid Barney. It was so successful we went back the following year with Benny Carter and Barney Bigard.

By now the Legends was a very lucrative band, and Crescent Jazz Productions was a thriving business. There was so much work we even operated an alternative band called Legends of Jazz Two. That band has Leo Dejan [Harold's brother] on trumpet and Floyd Turnham on saxophone. He later joined the number one band and was the best tenor player I ever worked with. He was also a fabulous man, but by God, he could drink. We called him Doc because he always carried a little case with a bottle each of bourbon, gin, vodka, and scotch, with cocktail shakers and mixers.

In February 1977, we went to Memphis with the Legends to play a concert. I had fixed with a local jazz and blues enthusiast, Harry Godwin, to interview some of the old blues musicians still living in Memphis. Henry agreed to drive me around and introduce me. When we got off the plane, around 7:00 a.m., he met us, and he took me to see Gus Cannon, who was the first one on my list; he was ninety-one years old at the time. It was a great interview, and I got it published in the English *Melody Maker.*

The bad news was Bukka White had died the day we arrived, and he was one of the ones I really wanted to interview. I called Furry Lewis, and he said, "Yeah, man, you can come over, but bring me some breakfast." I said, "What, like go to Denny's and get some ham and eggs?" He said, "Ham and eggs? Man, what I need is a pint of Ten High!" So I went to the liquor store and got the man his bourbon; it made another great interview.

Talking of blues musicians, I fixed to record Sunnyland Slim in San Francisco. A friend of mine let us use the Steinway grand in his house.

He wanted a fifth of bourbon, and he had brought a little black girl with him, real nice looking. Sunnyland said to my wife, "How do you like this girl—good looking, ain't she? But she's not as good a fuck as her sister!"

Around about 1977, I had the idea of writing a book about Barney. When I told him about the idea, he was already in failing health. I convinced him to do it by pointing out that if anything happened to him, his wife Dottie would get a share of the royalties. Interviewing him was like pulling teeth. He was very reticent, but it was fascinating. He hated rereading the material after it was transcribed. But eventually the book [With Louis and the Duke] was published.

We did a charity job for the Toys for Tots at the Beverley Wilshire Hotel, and Barney did a guest appearance with us. Rich people bring their toys, and the charity boxes and distributes them to underprivileged kids. The concert was to consist of Engelbert Humperdinck, Helen Reddy, and us. It was hosted by John Wayne.

Working with him was a peculiar experience. I can't explain it but you just knew he was in the room. He had an all-encompassing presence. You just felt he was there. The only other people in my life that had this presence were Louis Armstrong and Marlene Dietrich. After the show I shook hands with him, and he said, "You know, I don't generally like jazz, but I sure enjoyed you guys."

On the day, Engelbert Humperdinck called to say he couldn't come, which left Helen Reddy topping the bill. Then she had a row backstage with her husband (who was also her manager) and stormed out. That left us to do the whole show, which we did, and got a standing ovation. From then on, we did that show every year.

I think it was Barbara who called *The Dinah Shore Show*, which went out nationwide in the afternoons. The producer, whose name was Donald Ross, called me. He asked if we would like to appear on the show; I said yes. I started to tell him who was in the band, and he said, "I don't care who's in the band, as long as you are." This was something new; mostly, people booked us because of the other guys in the band.

We got our instructions from the show and went there. With something like that, you reach more people in a single afternoon than in five years of doing one-nighters round the U.S. While we were unloading the bus, a man came up and said, "Barry, great to see you again! I'm Donald

Ross." He put his arms round me and gave me two Romeo and Juliet cigars. I asked him where we'd met before, and he said, "I was working on the movie *Tom Jones* in England. I read in the paper that Don Ewell was at the 100 Club with your band. I spoke to you, and you were so nice to me. You introduced me to Don Ewell. Took me to a curry restaurant afterwards, paid for my meal, and gave me a ride back to my hotel." I said I didn't remember any of that, and he said, "That doesn't matter. I do, and that's why you're here."

He introduced me to Dinah Shore. She was very nice and looked great. The guests on the show were Charlton Heston, Vanessa Redgrave, and Claude Akins.

We went on and played two or three numbers, and she interviewed us. Then she said, "Can I sing a number with you?" We weren't expecting this, and it was live TV. She wanted to do "Sweet Georgia Brown" in C, and that's what we did. We closed the show with "Legends of Boogie" with Claude Akins and Dinah Shore jitterbugging.

The next day, I went to my usual cigar store, National Cigar, and the salesman said, "I saw you on *The Dinah Shore Show* yesterday. Are you famous? Let me get the boss, Mr. Bert." Mr. Bert came out and said, "Can we put your picture on the showroom wall?" (They already had pictures of Groucho Marx and George Burns.) I gave them a picture to display, and they gave me a third discount off my cigars.

Then I had a call from a guy called David Moorhead, who I knew through him coming with his wife to see the band. He wanted me to go down to his office, which was on Sunset Boulevard. While I was there, he called Johnny Carson and asked if he'd take us on *The Tonight Show*.

He set it up for us, and we went to do the show. Ed McMahon said to us, "We only want you to do one number. Johnny's a drummer and he would love to play with you." I said, "We've only got one number, it's my band, and I'm the drummer. No, I'd rather not do the show." They took it well, and I played drums.

Floyd and I organized the Los Angeles Jazz Festival, which ran for three nights and was completely sold out. On the second night, Joe Venuti[38] topped the bill. He was on stage, and Barney Bigard was in the front row of the audience. Joe announced from the stage, "Ladies and gentlemen, I want to acknowledge one of the real jazz greats, Mr. Barney Bigard, right here in the front row." Barney stood up and took a bow, everyone applauded, and when he sat down again, Joe looked at him and said, "Did you pay to get in?"

Later in the seventies, Floyd and I dissolved the partnership. The band was on the road all the time, and he couldn't travel with us. It was basically too much work for him. I kept ownership of the company, and Floyd took the records we had made, of which there were about six. In later years, the record label was sold to George Buck of the GHB Foundation, who reissued them.

We took the Legends of Jazz up to Canada for a promoter called Gerry Vineberg. He was a young guy but very progressive. It was one of the last tours that Floyd came on. We played Walla Walla, the Washington state pen, and Seattle, and barnstormed over to Winnipeg, via Banff, Calgary, and Edmonton. The tour ended on the Tuesday before Thanksgiving. Blake, Nelson, and Dolph flew home from there. Alton, Sam Lee, and I drove back. The towns are few and far between up there, and the sign in Little Gulch said "Next town, Bowman, 214 miles." When we got to Bowman on Thanksgiving Day, the next town was 340 miles, and we needed to fill up with gas—we didn't have nearly enough to make it.

There was nobody on the street, restaurants closed, gas station closed, it was like the start of a weird film. Finally, I spotted some lights on in a movie theater, and when I went in there, there was a lady cleaning the place. I asked her why there wasn't anyone around, and she said, "Everyone's up at the judge's place for the town Thanksgiving party." She phoned the Judge's place, and the local motel owner came down and checked us in. I asked him about restaurants, but there was nowhere open, and both the town's gas stations were closed until the following day. But the motel owner was kind enough to leave us a bag of quarters before he went back to the party, and our Thanksgiving dinner consisted of potato chips and candy bars from the vending machine. The next day, the gas station opened at 6:00 a.m., and we left town five minutes later.

The next year, we did the same tour again, this time in spring. We took Barney with us, but he was so sick he played his clarinet sitting in a wheelchair. It was obviously his last tour.

Earl Hines came to Los Angeles to play at Shelly's Manne-Hole. Tudi and I went to hear him, with our wives. Tudi said, "I'm Ed Garland. Tell that boy Hines to come out here. I'm not fixin' to pay!" It caused a bit of a ruckus, until I put a fifty-dollar bill in the woman's hand and winked at her. Tudi was blind, he couldn't see what was going on, and she said, "OK, Mr. Garland, you can go in." That satisfied him.

Inside, Earl Hines was playing to about ten people. I got talking to the owner, Shelly Manne. He was a really nice guy, and obviously disappointed at the low turn out. I got on the phone to Floyd the next day, and we rang damn near everyone on our mailing list. The following evening Shelly's was packed out.

The next time Earl Hines came to L.A. was at the Playboy Club. Barney and I went over to his motel, where he agreed to contribute the introduction to the book I was writing about Barney. The next day I went to the National Cigar, where they still had my picture on the wall, and got them to make up a box of cigars with "Earl Hines—World's Greatest Piano Player" printed on the cellophane. I took them to the Playboy Club and gave them to him in his dressing room. I don't think he smoked one of them; he was a little on the vain side.

Barney went into hospital, and Barbara and I went to see him there. His wife, Dottie, had been there for about twenty-four hours straight, and she went to get some rest. I was sitting holding Barney's hand. He could hardly move, but he managed to point to a ring on his finger, which I knew had belonged to his mother. I took it off and gave it to Dottie later. I guess Barney was concerned that the undertaker might get it. He couldn't speak, but when I took the ring, he nodded, closed his eyes, and died. His death took a lot of motivation out of the Los Angeles community.

A promoter called Mel Howard heard us at the Bijou Theatre on Broadway. He had a company called International Festival and Ballet, a booking agency operating out of New York. He called and mostly talked to Barbara, who had taken over the bookings since Floyd left. She'd met him at a booking agents' convention somewhere. Mel had the idea of amalgamating the Legends of Jazz with a tap dance troupe he was managing, called the Original Hoofers, and calling the show "1000 Years of Jazz." The name came from the combined ages of the band and the dancers, who were Harlem tap dancers, all in their seventies and eighties.

Mel got it together, and the Legends had to go to New York City for a meeting. We stayed at the George Washington Hotel, and Clyde Bernhardt joined us there. I got up early in the morning to see the worst blizzard New York had ever seen—the snow was a foot deep in Manhattan. We had to get to the Diplomat Hotel, where we were supposed to rehearse, but everywhere was paralyzed.

Mel turned up at about ten past eight, wearing a big Russian hat and overcoat, looking like he had come direct from Siberia. I noticed that he was limping, and asked if he'd fallen in the snow. "No," he said. "Infantile paralysis." Very matter of fact, no trace of self-pity. We managed to get one cab and sent it ahead with the drums. The rest of us walked down there through the snow; it was about twelve city blocks, but we made it. Mel introduced me to his secretary, Miss Plumley (who eventually became my third wife), and Eugene Lowry, who was to be stage manager.

We set up and played "Panama" for them. They were very enthusiastic. Then in came four guys carrying little bags. There was Lon Chaney (whose real name was Isaiah Chaneyfield), Raymond Kaalund (whose people came from Denmark), and Chuck Green. Lon Chaney asked if we knew "Perdido," and we started up; he danced. Raymond Kaalund had an eccentric dance style, and we played "Satin Doll" for him. Then it came to this little guy who said, "I'm Ralph Brown. I'm happy to be here, joy to the world! Do you boys know 'April in Paris'?" I said yes, expecting him to rehearse his dance routine, but he just said "Good, that's alright." and left. Mel told me that Ralph Brown was one of the biggest things on the bill. He had been master of ceremonies at the Cotton Club and subsequently been Jimmie Lunceford's tap dancer for several years.

Chuck Green was the most famous of all of them, and he wanted "Take the A Train" but very slow. He went into this routine like a ballet. He was the best tap dancer I've ever worked with.

We went on working out routines with the dancers; it was a completely new experience for me. Another dancer called Buster Brown turned up with his own arrangement of "Cute." It was just the lead and the chords, nothing special about it. He was a little bitty guy. Chaney was big, Raymond Kaalund was small, and Chuck Green was about six foot three.

Mel was pleased with what we'd done and sent everyone home. Ten days later, he called to say we would open in Quebec City, then play Rimouski, Trois Rivieres, and Montreal. I thought, "This is great, but what the hell are we going to do? We haven't got a show, just from that one rehearsal."

We went back to New York, and Mel called me at our hotel. He said,

"Have you seen any Zulus at your hotel? I'm running Zulu Macbeth in New York. . . ." His company was called International Festival and Ballet, and he would introduce American audiences to fire dancers from Thailand, and the Whirling Dervishes of Africa. I think the Thousand Years show was the first American art he had ever booked.

The next morning, we got onto a rented Greyhound bus—five dancers, six musicians, and a girl whose stage name was Mocha Java. Her real name was Denise De Lapena, and she was to be our vocalist. We worked out her repertoire on the bus to Quebec.

I was still apprehensive, we had no script, no stage routines, no plot, and we were to open at eight o'clock on the day we arrived. But when it came to it, that show just worked out itself, I don't know how.

We played the first three numbers. Then the girl did her routines, and then the dancers came on. The audience went bananas. There was no big directorial input.

The next day we got back on the bus, and I found myself sitting next to Miss Plumley, whose name turned out to be Norma. I told her it was my birthday, and she offered to buy me lunch. The following day I made arrangements to sit next to her on the bus. The first night in Montreal, we had a night off. I took her out for dinner at an Indian restaurant. We passed the building I used to live in on St. Marc Street, and we went in and had a look around for old times' sake. Things between us developed from there.

A couple of weeks later, the show had a two-week run at the Entermedia Theater, on New York's Lower East Side, right opposite the Stuyvesant Casino. The first night was sold right out, but I know [Mel had] given away a lot of free tickets. Afterwards, we went to Sardi's to wait for the reviews in the morning newspapers, which came about 4:00 a.m. The *New York Daily News* had a big picture of Blake with the caption "Blakeney's Horn of Plenty" and a great review. Clive Barnes gave us a great review in the *New York Times*. None of these people were musical—they were theater critics.

By the time we got to the theater the following night, Mel had got the reviews blown up and plastered on sandwich boards all over the place.

From then on, we did great business, going from strength to strength. We got friendly with the dancers, and we went to Puerto Rico, Martinique, all the Caribbean islands. After a while, Buster Brown left, and we replaced him with George Hillman, who was seventy years old when he joined us. All of those dancers had their own individual styles; they were kind of like jazz musicians in that respect.

We had a succession of girl singers, selected through what they call a "cattle call" in show business. Mel would put an announcement in *Billboard* or *Variety*. The girls would turn up and audition, sometimes forty at a time. They would issue them with numbered cloakroom tickets and call them up in order. Mel and the backers would sit in the third row smoking cigars, just like in the movies. All the girls wanted to sing Billie Holiday's song "God Bless the Child." Now I can't stand that song, even if Billie Holiday's singing it. Some of the girls wouldn't reach eight bars before they got "OK, that's enough! Number twenty next."

Mel also hired a very good singer called Linny Godfrey, who later made it big on TV. She would come on stage laying on a chaise longue, singing "Oh Daddy!" Eugene Lowry and a couple of the stagehands had to pull her on a rope. Eugene really took care of business; he contributed a lot towards the success of the show. Anyone at all who gave us any trouble, he gave them hell.

Lon Chaney was a tough nut; he'd been bodyguard to Sammy Davis Jr. He had a massive scar where he had taken a shotgun blast when he was running the numbers racket in Harlem. After he'd been shot, he'd beaten four guys to a pulp, put them in intensive care at the hospital. Raymond Kaalund left next, he used to drink twenty hours a day. Jimmy Slyde joined after Raymond left. He was a great dancer.

During the show's run at the Entermedia Theater, someone in the audience complained about the smell of pot that was wafting from the direction of the stage. Mel Howard came backstage looking for the source, which was the dancers' dressing room. Then he said, "I believe I can smell whiskey on someone's breath." Blakeney told him, "How dare you! We're professional musicians, we don't drink alcohol during a performance." Mel apologized and left, and Blake and I got our bottle of Jack Daniel's back out of the fire bucket.

We were up in the Adirondacks, Elmira, New York, playing in the open air to six thousand people. During the intermission, I saw our singer, Deborah Woodson, talking to a big black dude, Peg Leg Bates, the one-legged dancer. He owned a hotel nearby, and he invited us all back after the show. But before that, he came on stage and danced with us during the second set. The idea of a one-legged tap dancer sounds ridiculous, but he used his peg leg as part of his routine. He was wonderful.

Before we got Deborah Woodson, we'd had a succession of singers who were really good looking but a pain in the ass. Deborah had turned up at the end of a cattle call and rocked the place with "Precious Lord." She stayed with us for about four years. She could sing anything you wanted to do, a thoroughly professional girl. She was hard, too. The two of us were coming out of Small's Paradise one night, and a couple of guys came with "Hey, beautiful! What you doing with this ugly white bastard?" She pulled a razor out of her purse and said, "I'll cut the nuts off you mother-fuckers. Get away from us." They ran off.

Blake got too old to tour, and I replaced him with the New Orleans trumpet player Herbert Permillion.

The dancers got together one time. They never did like Alton Purnell's piano playing—they preferred swing style. Mel called me up to the office and said he wanted to replace Alton, and would that be a problem? I said it wouldn't, but it seemed a shame, because we'd had a good run. He looked relieved, and said, "That's great, so I can tell the dancers that you're will-ing to fire Purnell?" I said, "I didn't say that. If he goes, the band goes." He asked, "What am I going to tell the dancers?" I said, "Tell them to stick it where the sun don't shine. Nobody hires and fires my band but me." So they decided to get used to Purnell.

We went to Costa Rica, Panama, Argentina, Chile, Columbia, Peru, and all across the U.S. We were in Chile for five weeks. We were due to do a short tour with Cab Calloway, but it never happened. His contract specified star treatment, including being met at the airport by a stretch limo. When he arrived, there was just a regular limo, so he turned round, got on the next flight home, and canceled the whole deal.

One time when we were in Germany, Sam Lee decided to wash the band bus. The water faucet was behind a tall bush, and Sam threw a bucket of cold water over the bush just as two German ladies were pass-ing. They got soaked and started screaming. Sam made things worse by rushing round the bush, shouting sorry, and trying to brush the water off them with his hands. They thought they were being raped and called the police. Sam was kicks!

Another thing he would do was finish what was on people's plates after they had left their restaurant table—he told us that eating this way saved him about eighty dollars a week. One diner in Argentina had left most of a steak on a plate, and Sam wasted no time in sitting down and tucking in. Then the man came back from the restroom to find Sam sitting at his table, eating his dinner. A vigorous discussion developed, Sam's side of which consisted of "Bow-wow."

In 1982, we did a five-week run at the Ford's Theater, Washington. It was a really prestigious place. Abraham Lincoln had been assassinated there. At the end of our run, the theater was booked for the President's Command Performance; Ronald Reagan was in office at the time. Liza Minnelli was on the bill, David Copperfield, Lou Rawls, and the U.S. Army choir.

On the day of the performance, we were invited to the White House for lunch. We had to rent tuxedos to go. Purnell refused to rent a tuxedo, so he never met the president. We had to go through metal detectors and strip searches going into the White House, where we ended up in a red room. Red carpet, walls, drapes—a bit like an Indian restaurant. A waiter with a powdered wig came up and said, "Mr. Martyn? Jack Daniel's with a water back, I believe sir." How the hell did he know what I drank? And he knew what everyone else drank too. They'd certainly done their research.

These big double doors opened and the president came in, shook my hand, and said, "I'm so pleased you could come."

Things weren't going too well between me and Barbara, and we went through an unhappy divorce. She got the gold mine and I got the shaft. I'd like to say I walked away with nothing, but actually I drove away with nothing. I got one car, and that was all I had. I was forty years old. It's all part of life's rich pageant.

I drove to New York, after I'd said good-bye to my friends and kissed the dog good-bye, up Route 66. It started snowing in Kingman, Arizona, and it didn't stop until I crossed the George Washington Bridge. Outside Amarillo, Texas, I had to stop the car to avoid a herd of stampeding Texas longhorns heading the wrong way up the freeway. The weather got so bad I checked into a motel in Amarillo. I was marooned there for three nights, and they ran out of everything except steak and bourbon. The local police were commandeering all four-wheel-drive vehicles. Then the blizzard lifted and I carried on to New York.

It's a strange city, I never liked it much. I went to Norma's apartment, on 111th and Broadway. The Thousand Years show was still going.

We were doing a job in Key West, Florida, and I was just going on stage. The company manager came to me and said, "We had a phone call. Your mother just died." I had to go out and sing "Oh, How I Miss You Tonight" to two thousand people. Why the hell they didn't have the brains to tell me after the show, I don't know.

We had one date left on the itinerary, which was at Key Largo. Mel Howard convinced me to do the job, and then he flew me to Miami by helicopter. From there I flew to England and arrived just in time for my mother's funeral.

It was a bit later on that Bill Russell reentered my life. We went to a concert by the New Orleans Ragtime Orchestra, went backstage, and the first dressing room we tried, there was Bill, all on his own, sawing away on the violin. It was great to see him again, and we sat and talked until was time for him to go back on stage. He amazed me, because he was aware of everything I'd done since we last met; the Legends of Jazz, the Barney Bigard book, everything. I was tickled pink.

Back in New York, I had a lot of time off between shows. On 113th Street, right where we lived, there was a place called the West End Café. Norma and I would walk the dog by there and listen. If the music was good, we'd take the dog home and come back. Dickie Wells had a band there with Earl Warren. Harold Ashby took a band in. Brooks Kerr had a trio with Russell Procope and Sonny Greer. The night Zutty died, Roy Eldridge came to the place, and Max Roach. It was just a place to congregate, but that was a sad night.

Jo Jones opened there. He had fixed to play with a quartet, with Harold Ashby on tenor, Ram Ramirez on piano, and Johnny Williams on bass. But he had screwed up the date of the opening, and when Norma and I got there, he was sitting on stage behind the drums by himself!

The club had to hire a couple of last-minute replacements for the band, and all they could get at short notice was a couple of college kids on bass and guitar. I never heard drums like that night. Jo really had to work hard to keep the two kids straight. You could have sent a hundred drummers down there, and they would have learned something. He's my favorite drummer in the world.

* * *

Norma and I got married in South Queensferry in Scotland. We went to the pub first, and I saw a bunch of Edinburgh musicians. There was Jim Petrie, Jim Young, Jack Wedell. I thought it was just coincidence. At the end of the ceremony the reverend said, "Excuse me a minute" and went out. Two minutes later, he came back playing tenor sax, leading a brass band. They paraded us all up the street.

Back in New York, I founded a trio with Lars Edegran and Orange Kellin, who were up there with the "One Mo' Time" show. We played at a place called the Cajun Restaurant, on Second Avenue. We used a singer called Ruth Brisbane. Then we started at the Village Gate on Sunday afternoons.

The problem was, every job in New York paid fifty dollars. The local musicians were working for that, and it was way below union scale. But it was enough to keep the wolf from the door. When Lars was out of town, we hired top replacements, like Eddy Durham on trombone and guitar.

By then the Thousand Years show was sort of winding down. The bookings got sparser because Mel was concentrating on a project called "Tango Argentina," which became a hit show in New York.

Norma and I took a trip down to New Orleans. We stayed on Elysian Fields, and I sat in with a few bands. The pull became too strong, and I realized that I wanted to come back to New Orleans. What finally decided it was, I had to do a three-month tour in Europe. When I came back to New York, Lars and Orange had put the word out they had fired me, which was absolutely not true.

1985–2004
NEW ORLEANS

By 1985, nearly all the old-time New Orleans musicians had passed on, and their art with them. But there was one aspect of their music that survived almost intact. In the early years of the twentieth century, brass bands had routinely used written music, particularly for the multithemed dirges performed at funerals. Fortunately, the musical notation for much of this dignified music of remembrance survives today and enables contemporary musicians to access the repertoire of bands like the Eureka and the Young Tuxedo in a particularly accurate way.

It's November 29, 2004. On the second-floor sundeck at Barry Martyn's house on Burgundy Street, there's a rehearsal of Andrew Hall's Society Brass Band. Barry's main musical interest nowadays is in brass band music, and it shows. We've been up for hours, pasting photocopied band parts on pieces of card, and it's still only ten in the morning. One by one, the musicians wander out onto the deck. Andrew Hall, a suave expatriate Englishman, is the band leader and snare drummer. Senior bandsman is the spry eighty-one-year-old Wendell Eugene, who played trombone with Lucky Millinder back in the forties. There's the superb musician Tom Fischer on the alto sax and part-time policeman and schoolteacher Joe Torregano on tenor. The trumpet players are Clive Wilson (another Englishman) and Chris Clifton, who once played with Lil Armstrong's band. Apologies for absence are phoned in by Edgar Smith— there's been a gun scare at his son's school, and the boy has been injured in the ensuing stampede.

Barry plays bass drum and effectively runs the rehearsal. The musicians, like musicians everywhere, are reluctant to actually start playing, so there's a lengthy discussion about the hymn *"Abide with Me"* and who should play the lead on which chorus.

Then it's time for the stately dirge *"Eternity,"* which Tom Fischer has scored for the band. It's a fairly complicated piece. Tom hasn't written any parts for the drummers, the tempo is ultraslow, and there are some problems with synchronizing everybody in the first two themes. But they finally get it down, and the beautiful last theme, with its mariachi-like trumpet voicing, mingles with the birdsong from the surrounding trees.

Next up is the brisk march "On the Square," followed by "Moose March," for which some of the band parts are missing. The trumpets and saxophones are reading, but unflappable veteran Wendell Eugene sits at an empty music stand, making up a perfect trombone part as he goes along.

Clarinetist Chris Burke arrives, explains that he can't play because he's hurt his finger, shows everyone the finger, and leaves. Surely a telephone call would have done the job?

When trumpet player Percy Humphrey led the Eureka band, he prevented bandsmen from stealing the repertoire by the simple expedient of cutting the titles off the music and substituting numbers. So the next rehearsal item, a beautiful slow hymn, has survived under the name "No. 452." As it rings out in the morning sunshine, a passing lady cyclist calls up to the deck, "That sounds good!" It certainly does.

So I moved back to New Orleans. I called my son Emile, and he flew out to New York to help me with the move. We loaded the stuff in a U-Haul truck and drove south. I didn't have anywhere to live, and my friend Chris Burke very kindly put me up for five weeks while I got myself together.

Then I bought the house we're sitting in now, 3621 Burgundy Street, just before Christmas 1984. There was a big freeze, all the pipes burst, and it cost me two thousand dollars to get them fixed.

I started working in a band led by Chris Burke. He had two nights at Storyville and three nights at the Gazebo. Both places are on Decatur Street, near the French Market. Plus we were doing outside jobs. The band settled down to a regular personnel: Wendell Brunious on trumpet, John Royen on piano, Chris, and me.

I noticed a lot of changes in New Orleans since I had last worked there. For one thing, the musicians played the blues much faster. The practice of playing ensemble had almost gone—it was all solos. There were a lot more European musicians, especially English. They all stuck together; it was like the Raj.

And there was a whole new generation of younger black musicians. For years people of my generation had been bemoaning the fact that there were no young black musicians coming up, but in 1985 there were people like Wendell Brunious, Freddy Lonzo, Gregg Stafford and Michael White. They'd all come up while I'd been in Los Angeles.

The Olympia band was still going strong, and there were a number of young modern brass bands. But nobody was playing the older style of brass band music which I heard when I first came to New Orleans. So I set about forming my own Eagle Brass Band. Harold Dejan agreed to join, and between us we had a lot of the scores from the old bands. I got Reggie Koeller, Milton Batiste, and Emery Thompson on trumpets. They worked for me if they didn't have a prior booking. I got Wendell Eugene on trombone and Big Al Carson on bass horn. Freddie Kemp came in on tenor sax and Gerry Anderson on snare drum. We started rehearsing and getting a few jobs.

We made a recording, and I used my old English trumpet player, Dan Pawson, along with Milton and Emery. Emery stopped the band and said, "One of us trumpets is making a wrong note in the second bar." Milton said, "Well, it ain't me, Em." Emery said, "I know." So who else would it be out of the three of them but Dan?

As time went by, Harold and Freddie Kemp died, and Big Al Carson couldn't walk anymore. So me and Wendell Eugene joined Andrew Hall's Society Brass Band, and that was the end of the Eagle band.

A bit later, we put together a cooperative band called the Young Men of New Orleans. We had Freddy Lonzo on trombone, Wendell Brunious on trumpet, Orange Kellin, clarinet. I asked Butch Thompson to play piano, but he was tied up with Garrison Keillor and *Prairie Home Companion*, the radio show.

Wendell and Freddy suggested we should try Ed Frank for the piano job. They told me he only had one hand. I'd never heard of Ed Frank, and I wondered what good a one-handed piano player could possibly be. When he turned up, I was amazed. I just couldn't see how anyone could play so much piano with one hand. I got McNeal Breaux on bass; he had moved back to New Orleans by then.

We made two European trips, but the tensions within the band broke it up. They got angry because promoters in Europe would advertise the band using my name. I never asked for it, but they probably figured that audiences over there knew me. Anyway, it gradually fell apart.

I carried on working in New Orleans for Chris Burke and Andrew Hall. Plus I would make a solo trip to Europe each year, playing in England, Belgium, and Italy.

I had recorded twenty MONO albums, and the last one I could afford to issue was Kid Thomas at the Tip Top, which was number eighteen. I decided to concentrate on tracking down sessions that I knew had been recorded but never issued rather than try and make more recording sessions. That intention wasn't realized until after I returned to New Orleans in 1985.

George Buck had moved down here, with his GHB label. He had been trying to buy the American music label for the longest time. I was there when they finally clinched the deal. George offered a certain number of dollars, and Bill refused. George said, "Well, that's the most I can offer." And Bill told him, "No, that's ridiculous. It's not worth that." They finally agreed a much lower sum, and Bill signed a contract.

George put Gus Statiras in charge of the project. Bill mapped out the first CD, which was called *Bunk Johnson, King of the Blues*. The record came out, and the sleeve note was riddled with spelling mistakes, starting with the first word—"Buck" Johnson. Bill was disgusted and withdrew from the project; he just lost interest and refused to participate.

George Buck was in a dilemma. The only man that could produce the project was now against it. He came to me and asked could I talk Bill into coming back. The board of directors was at the time George Buck, Rudi Blesh, Art Hodes, Wendell Echolls, me, and Bill Russell. I figured a strategy that I knew would work.

I went to see Bill and said to him, "Look, Bill. We can't do this American Music thing without you. You're on the board of directors, and you signed a piece of paper saying you would help the company's interests. The company needs your loyalty, irrespective of any personal squabbles. I know you're an honorable man; you can't renege on your responsibility. You know what you've got to do; otherwise you're joining the ranks of dishonorable bastards we've all had to deal with on a daily basis. Let's get it over with. Are you going to do it or not?"

He said, "Oh gee, what else can I do when you put it like that?" We shook hands on it, and I told him I'd be working with him. He had planned and mapped out a further five CDs. We trusted each other, and we took it from there. We had a lot of arguments, but they were always constructive. I once said to him, "Why did you record all this music?" He said, "That's easy to answer. It was the best music I'd ever heard."

I was amazed at the amount and variety of music that he had recorded. Gradually, we listened to all of it. There was a session from August 1944 on which Bunk Johnson was obviously drunk and below par. We managed to salvage some of it by judicious editing. We worked together really well; we were friends and we both shared the same objectives.

Then George Buck acquired the Oxford series of recordings, featuring the George Lewis band. We decided to issue them on American Music, in addition to the ten CDs that Bill had originally planned. There was other stuff that I wanted to issue on the label, magnifying Bill's work and bringing in other people's work where it seemed appropriate.

I discussed the idea with Bill, and he agreed. What he actually said was "I trust your judgment." After that, we had phenomenal scope. We had my material from the MONO series, there was a lot of stuff recorded by Dr. Herbert Otto, there was Ken Mills's Icon label, there were various acetates of radio broadcasts that Bill had collected. We couldn't have done any of this without George Buck's backing.

Bill's material made twenty-one CDs. After the first five, tragedy struck—Bill got sick. His niece Lois took him out to Slidell to take care of him. When he came back from there, the International Association of Jazz Record Collectors were coming to New Orleans. They planned to honor Bill, and he didn't want to go. On the day of the event, he called me and said he'd changed his mind and asked if I would give him a ride over there. He slipped and fell the same day, didn't attend the event, and died shortly afterwards. He left instructions for what I had to do next.

There were several institutions vying for his collection, including the Smithsonian Institution and the Historic New Orleans Collection. His brother William and I went through Bill's stuff and sorted it into three piles. One was American Music stuff, one was personal, and the third was for the collection. Anything else was junk, and we put it into a big garbage can outside. It was rifled through by jazz fans. After that, we took about two loads of garbage up to my house.

We went to see the Historic Collection, and Dick Allen came with us. Hurricane Andrew was about to hit, and I asked the Historic Collection board what facilities they had to protect the material from hurricanes.

They showed me the security vaults, and it was like a bank vault. We decided to give them the collection; the security was so good, and it seemed right that it should stay in New Orleans.

I now had all the masters, and I had to make all the decisions. My guiding light was to ask myself what Bill would have done. It sounds a bit morbid, but I still ask him questions now. I've now done 120 CDs in the series.

I've also single-handedly run Jazzology Press, and we've now issued ten books, as well as two collections of films on video. The first American Music video featured Baby Dodds. The film had no soundtrack, but I was able to painstakingly construct one from music I already owned. Then I made *Sing On* about the old brass bands, which I coproduced with my friend Richard Knowles.

Around 1995, I had a letter from the Department of the Interior. The National Park Service was going to declare the whole town of New Orleans a National Jazz Park. They had selected me to be a Jazz Commissioner. They had a very good superintendent named Gayle Hazelwood. I told her I wanted to concentrate on an interview program for New Orleans musicians. She saw the importance of it, and so far, Jack Stewart and I have interviewed 116 people between us.

The interviews were made on videotape, and they last about two hours each. It's a big plus to be able to see the subject as they're talking, and once in a while they would bring their instruments and play a little bit. They're incredibly informative about all kinds of New Orleans music.

Unlike Bill Russell, I don't have anybody in New Orleans waiting in the wings to succeed me. If I don't get this work done, I doubt if it will ever be done.

I suppose I've led a full life. Played with and heard all kind of musicians and entertainers. I've been truly blessed. I'd do exactly the same thing over if I was given a chance. I have two sons, both of them musicians, and I get a kick watching them do the same stuff I did. I've been leading a band for fifty years, and right now I have a band called the Young Bloods. I have lots of music in me that has to come out yet. I have more mountains to climb. I live quietly on Burgundy Street with my girlfriend, Karen. Still write books, and produce CDs and whatever. I am happy and my philosophy is "Reach for the moon and you might grab the stars. If you reach for the ceiling, you'll be lucky to get out of your armchair."

Appendix 1

Barry Martyn Collection of Interviews, Historic New Orleans Collection

Watkins, Joe, drums, Jan. 20, 1961
Cola, George "Kid Sheik," trumpet, Jan. 28, 1961
Sayles, Emanuel, banjo, Jan. 29, 1961
Williams, Alfred, drums, Feb. 3, 1961
Frazier, Cié, drums, Feb. 16, 1961
Bigard, Alex, drums, Feb. 7, 1962
Dawson, Eddie, bass, Jan. 31, 1962
Bocage, Peter, trumpet, 1962
Barnes, Emile, clarinet, Feb. 7, 1962
Handy, John, saxophone, Nov. 21, 1963
Summers, Eddie, trombone, Nov. 11, 1963
Kelly, Jack (son of Chris), Nov. 17, 1963
Crescent City Crystals, various, Nov. 13, 1963
Ferbos, Lionel, trumpet, Aug. 3, 1964
Cola, "Kid Shiek," on Chris Kelly, 1963
Dejan, Harold, saxophone, March 28, 1963
Morgan, Andrew, saxophone, March 20, 1969
Barnes, Paul, saxophone, June 16, 1969
Kimball, Jeanette, piano, June 19, 1969
Valentine, "Kid" Thomas, trumpet, June 17, 1969
Tio, Rose (Lorenzo Tio's daughter), July 7, 1969
Hamilton, Charles, piano, 1969
Maurice, Emile, drums, 1969
Williams, Peter, drums, 1969
Franklin, Henry "Dog," clarinet, 1969
Blunt, Cal, trombone, Nov. 23, 1963
Murray, Frank, guitar, 1969
McNeil, John Henry, trumpet, 1969
Moore, Buster, trombone, 1969
Spears, E., saxophone, 1969
Purnell, Alton, piano, 1970
Humphrey, Percy, trumpet, 1970

Thompson, Leroy, trumpet, 1971

Gallaud, Louis, piano, 1971

Murphy, Turk, trombone, Dec. 1, 1972

Hines, Earl, piano, 1973

Bechet, Leonard, saxophone, Dec. 4, 1972

Delay, Mike, trumpet, Jan. 19, 1973

Alcorn, Alvin, trumpet, 1993

Koeller, Reginald, trumpet, 1995

Potier, Harold, trumpet, Sept. 20, 1995

Veasey, Paul, Sept. 20, 1995

Viltz, Leander (Bunk coworker, rice mill), Sept. 21, 1995

Polk, Matthew (sponsored WPA program for Bunk), Sept. 21, 1995

Blumberg, Jerry, trumpet (Bunk's student), Oct. 25, 1993

Dejan, Leo, Nov. 25, 1991

Otto, Herbert, Aug. 6, 1992

Broun, Heywood Hale, n.d.

Pierce, De De (interviewed by Dick Allen), n.d.

Pierce, Billie (interviewed by Dick Allen), n.d.

Butler, Joseph "Kid Twat" (interviewed by Dick Allen), n.d.

Gorman, Israel (interviewed by Dick Allen), n.d.

Leo Dejan, n.d.

Harold Dejan, 1998

Harold Potier and John Fontennette, 1996

Walter Lewis, 1997

Milford Doliole video, original 8-mm film of Cié Frazier and
    Alfred Williams, 1986

William Wagner, n.d.

Harry Newmark, n.d.

Bill Bowler, n.d.

Earl Hines, piano, n.d.

Appendix 2

American Music Reissue Program

AMCD-01	Bunk: King of the Blues
AMCD-02	George Lewis, Kid Shots Madison
AMCD-03	Bunk Johnson, 1944
AMCD-04	George Lewis Trios
AMCD-05	Wooden Joe Nicholas
AMCD-06	Bunk's Brass Band
AMCD-07	Big-Eye Louis Nelson
AMCD-08	Bunk, 1944: Second Masters
AMCD-09	Herb Morand
AMCD-10	Kid Thomas: The First Recordings
AMCD-11	Dink Johnson, Charlie Thompson
AMCD-12	Bunk, 1944–45
AMCD-13	Emile Barnes
AMCD-14	Mobile Strugglers
AMCD-15	Bunk Plays Popular Songs
AMCD-16	Bunk in San Francisco
AMCD-17	Baby Dodds: Drum Record
AMCD-18	Natty Dominique Creole Dance Band
AMCD-19	Kid Ory,1944–46
AMCD-20	Kid Ory, 1948–49
AMCD-21	Oxford Vol. 1: Lewis, 1952 Party
AMCD-22	Oxford Vol. 2: Lewis, 1952 Concert
AMCD-23	Oxford Vol. 3: Lewis, 1952 Concert
AMCD-24	Oxford Vol. 4: Lewis, 1953 Rec.
AMCD-25	Oxford Vol. 5: Lewis, 1953 1st Concert
AMCD-26	Oxford Vol. 6: Lewis, 1953 1st Concert
AMCD-27	Oxford Vol. 7: Lewis, 1953 2nd Concert
AMCD-28	Oxford Vol. 8: Lewis, 1953 2nd Concert
AMCD-29	Oxford Vol. 9: Lewis, 1953 Ves/Reh/Party
AMCD-30	Oxford Vol. 10: Lewis, 1955 Party
AMCD-31	Oxford Vol. 11: Lewis, 1955 Concert
AMCD-32	Oxford Vol. 12: Lewis, 1955 Concert

AMCD-33	Oxford Vol. 13: Lewis and Lucas, 1955
AMCD-34	Oxford Vol. 14: Lewis and Lucas, 1955
AMCD-35	Oxford Vol. 15: Barbarin, 1956 Concert
AMCD-36	Oxford Vol. 16: Barbarin, 1956 Concert
AMCD-37	Oxford Vol. 17: Spirituals in Ragtime
AMCD-38	George Lewis Band with Elmer Talbert, 1949–50
AMCD-39	Fabulous G. Lewis Band, Kentucky 1956
AMCD-40	Kid Howard: Prelude to the Revival
AMCD-41	Kid Rena: Prelude to the Revival, Vol. 2
AMCD-42	Kid Ory: Green Room, Vol. 1
AMCD-43	Kid Ory: Green Room, Vol. 2
AMCD-44	John Reid Collection
AMCD-45	Bunk and Mutt Carey, New York
AMCD-46	Bunk and Leadbelly, New York
AMCD-47	Ray Burke's Speakeasy Boys
AMCD-48	Kid Thomas: The Dance Hall Years
AMCD-49	Kid Thomas: Slatter Recordings
AMCD-50	Big Boy Goudie
AMCD-51	John Handy: The First Recordings
AMCD-52	Punch Miller, 1960
AMCD-53	Kid Thomas: Sonnets from Algiers
AMCD-54	Kid Howard's La Vida Band
AMCD-55	Paul Barnes's Polo Players
AMCD-56	Steve Angrum, George Lewis
AMCD-57	Punch Miller, Delegates of Pleasure
AMCD-58	Kid Howard Olympia and Morgan Bands
AMCD-59	Creole George Guesnon, George Lewis
AMCD-60	Charlie Love
AMCD-61	John Casimir, Young Tuxedo Band
AMCD-62	Kid Clayton's Happy Pals
AMCD-63	Emile Barnes
AMCD-64	Billie and De De Pierce
AMCD-65	Alvin Acorn's Gay Paree Serenaders
AMCD-66	Albert Warner, Albert Jiles
AMCD-67	New Orleans Dance Bands
AMCD-68	Punch Miller, Louis Gallaud
AMCD-69	Kid Sheik in Boston and Cleveland
AMCD-70	Eureka Brass Band, 1951
AMCD-71	George Lewis, Red Allen
AMCD-72	Mutt Carey, Lee Collins
AMCD-73	Lizzie Miles

AMCD-74	George Lewis at Herbert Otto's Party
AMCD-75	Zenith BB, Eclipse Alley, Avery Tillman
AMCD-76	Billie Pierce, Ray Burke
AMCD-77	Brunies Brothers
AMCD-78	Johnny St. Cyr
AMCD-79	Billie and De De Solo, Binghamton
AMCD-80	Billie and De De Solo, Binghamton
AMCD-81	Billie and De De Band, Binghamton
AMCD-82	Billie and De De Band, Binghamton
AMCD-83	George Lewis Trios, Bands, etc.
AMCD-84	Barnes, Bocage Big Five
AMCD-85	George Lewis at Manny's Tavern, 1949
AMCD-86	Opening Night at Preservation Hall
AMCD-87	Creole George Guesnon
AMCD-88	Percy Humphrey Sympathy Five
AMCD-89	Buster Wilson, 1947–49
AMCD-90	Kid Ory at Crystal Pier
AMCD-91	Kid Sheik's Swingsters
AMCD-92	Kid Howard (MONO)
AMCD-93	Peter Bocage Creole Serenaders
AMCD-94	Emile and Polo Barnes, Louis Cottrell
AMCD-95	Olympia and Eureka (MONO)
AMCD-96	Gibson Brass Band (MONO)
AMCD-97	Kid Thomas at the Tip Top
AMCD-98	Crescent City Crystals Dance
AMCD-99	Mighty Four at Melody Inn
AMCD-100	Climax Sessions, Vol. 1
AMCD-101	Climax Sessions, Vol. 2
AMCD-102	Emile Barnes
AMCD-103	Joe Darensbourg, Dixie Flyers
AMCD-104	George Lewis Jam Session (Paradox)
AMCD-105	George "Pops" Foster, Art Hodes
AMCD-106	Herb Morand with Paul Barbarin
AMCD-107	George Lewis in Congo Square
AMCD-108	Raymond and Parenti with Lewis Band
AMCD-109	Muggsy Spanier in New Orleans, 1938–55
AMCD-110/1	Eureka Brass Band (Sam Charters)
AMCD-112	George Lewis at Castle Farm
AMCD-113	Dance Hall Days, Vol. 1
AMCD-114	Dance Hall Days, Vol. 2
AMCD-115	Kid Thomas, 1957: Dancing Tonight

AMCD-116	Bunk, 1945 Deccas
AMCD-117	Kid Thomas and Raymond Burke
AMCD-118	Love-Jiles Ragtime Orchestra in Rehearsal
AMCD-119	Bunk: Jazz Informations
AMCD-120	Big-Eye Louis Nelson: Second Masters
AMVD-01	Baby Dodds: New Orleans Drumming
AMVD-02	Sing On: Brass Bands

Appendix 3

Interviewees of the National Park Service Interview Program

Adams, Placide
Alcorn, Alvin
Allen, Richard B.
Arlt, Helen
Badie, Peter "Chuck"
Batiste, Lawrence E.
Batiste, Lionel
Batiste, Milton
Battiste, Harold
Bauduc, Alexander
Bell, Warren, Sr.
Bigard, Barney
Bigard, Dorothe (Mrs. Barney)
Black, Claire
Boudreaux, John
Breaux, McNeal
Broussard, Al
Castigliola, Sal
Chase, Dooky
Clifton, Chris
Cook, Olivia-Charlot
Cotton, Lawrence
Crosby, Richard L.
Dalmado, Tony
Darois, Philip
Davis, Gregory
Dejan, Harold
Dejan, Leo
DeVore, Charlie
Draghetti, Marguerite Laine
Eugene, Wendell
Farrow, Daniel

Fasnacht, Dixie
Ferbos, Lionel
Gailodoro, Al
Gallagher, John
Gallagher, M. G.
Gardner, Albert "June"
Gaspard, Charlie
Gaspard, Corrinne "Cookie," and
  Rose Tio
Gordon, Regina
Grisaffi, Joseph
Hardesty, Herbert
Herrmann, Paul J.
Huntington, Bill
Johnson, Joseph
Jones, Benny, Sr.
Joseph, Waldron "Frog"
Kimball, Narvin
King, Eddie
Koeller, Reginald
Lambert, Phamous
Levin, Floyd
Lewis, Walter
Luft, George
Mancuso, Vincent H.
Manone, Joseph, Jr.
Marquis, Donald M.
Matassa, Cosimo
Maxwell, Edward J.
Metcalf, Willie, Jr.
Meyer, Norman A.
Mielke, Bob

Minyard, Norma Dugas
Mitchell, Curtis
Mitchell, Frank
Mooney, Sam
Morris, Adolphus
Nunez, Eugene
Palmer, Earl
Payne, Richard
Payton, Walter
Permillion, Herbert
Perry, Don
Phillips, Inez
Quaglino, Joe
Ramos, Lamar A., Jr.

Rosato, Frank J.
Schmidt, Henry G.
Schrenk, Harley C.
Sheppard, Frederick
Smith, Edgar
Suter, Allen David
Thornton, Clarence
Torregano, Joseph
Vicari, Frank
Wagner, William
Washington, Lloyd
Watson, Ernest J., Jr.
Weaver, Mrs. Peter
White, Michael

Notes

1. George Lewis (Joseph Francois Zenon), clarinet (July 13, 1900–December 31, 1968). Made his first recordings for a small independent record company in the early 1940s and went on to become an international star, filling concert halls all over the world until his death. His playing was characterized by a delicate fragility, a huge tone, and enormous emotional sincerity.

2. Nathan "Jim" Robinson, trombone (December 25, 1892–May 4, 1976). Had recorded with the celebrated Sam Morgan band in New Orleans in 1927, before coming to the attention of a wider audience (along with George Lewis) in the Bunk Johnson band. His international fame was linked to that of Lewis, with whom he is most often associated. His musical approach is perhaps best described as "forthright," but no other trombonist could drive a band like Jim Robinson.

3. George "Kid Sheik" Cola, trumpet (September 15, 1908–November 7, 1996). Although not the best trumpet player in New Orleans, Sheik was a performer of great charm and personal amiability. He embodied the qualities of New Orleans musicians of his generation.

4. Percy Gaston Humphrey, trumpet (January 13, 1905–July 22, 1995). Grandson of "Professor" James Humphrey, who, beginning in the 1880s, had traveled the rural areas of Louisiana forming and teaching brass bands. Percy Humphrey joined the celebrated Eureka Brass Band in the 1920s, finally taking over the leadership in 1947. In recordings of the Eureka band, he soars over the out-choruses like a bird in flight.

5. Peter Edwin Bocage, trumpet and violin (July 31, 1887–December 3, 1967). A highly accomplished and respected musician, he recorded with the A. J. Piron orchestra in the 1920s, for which he also wrote compositions and arrangements. He made radio broadcasts in Boston with Sidney Bechet and added his own formal and more "legitimate" flavor to the New Orleans revival.

6. Arthur James "Zutty" Singleton, drums (May 14, 1898–July 14, 1975). Regarded as one of the best drummers ever to come out of New Orleans, Singleton left the city in 1924 and made a series of legendary recordings with Louis Armstrong in 1928. His matchless drive won him a place in bands not associated with New Orleans. He recorded with Roy Eldridge in the 1930s and with Dizzy Gillespie and Charlie Parker in the 1940s.

7. Alex Bigard, drums (March 3, 1899–June 27, 1978). Brother of the much more famous Barney, he stayed in New Orleans, and like Cié Frazier, played with the orchestras of A. J. Piron, John Robichaux, and Sidney Desvigne. Made his first recording at the age of fifty-three and was forced to quit playing in 1969 by increasing deafness.

8. Albany Leon "Barney" Bigard, clarinet (March 3, 1906–June 27, 1980). Left New Orleans in 1924 to join King Oliver in Chicago. Most famous for his fifteen-year stint as

featured soloist with Duke Ellington's orchestra (1927–1942). Sporadically played with Kid Ory's band and then with Louis Armstrong's All Stars from 1947 until 1961. One of the all-time great jazz clarinetists, his playing is notable for a limpid "woody" sound and dazzling technical facility.

9. Albert Burbank, clarinet (March 25, 1902–August 15, 1976). Another fine musician who came to wider attention late in his career—in his case, because of his first recordings in 1945. Although his musical reputation was largely eclipsed by George Lewis, George regarded him as a serious rival.

10. "Kid" Thomas Valentine, trumpet (February 3, 1896–June 16, 1987). Musically active on New Orleans's West Bank as early as the 1920s, he was first recorded in the 1950s, both with his own rumbustious dance band and with George Lewis. One of the most instantly recognizable of trumpet players, his minimalist style gave him the reputation of a "primitive," which belied his sly humor and innate musicality.

11. Avery "Kid" Howard, trumpet (April 22, 1908–March 28, 1966). Musically active from 1924 but attracted international acclaim as the trumpet player on the George Lewis Climax session in 1943. Although he later made recordings under his own name, he was known chiefly because of his long association with the George Lewis band.

12. Harold "Duke" Dejan, saxophone (February 4, 1909–July 5, 2002). By no means a virtuoso, Harold was a man of great charm, charisma, and popularity who worked steadily as a band leader and sideman throughout his career. Besides, he once told me, "I have always found plenty of work because of my ability to read music."

13. Josiah "Cié" Frazier, drums (February 23, 1904–January 10, 1985). A schooled musician, Cié played with most of the top New Orleans dance bands: A. J. Piron's, John Robichaux's, Oscar Celestin's, and Sidney Desvigne's. From a well-known New Orleans family, he was related to Philip and Keith Frazier of the contemporary Rebirth Brass Band.

14. "Creole" George Guesnon, banjo and guitar (May 25, 1907–May 5, 1968). Played with the famous Sam Morgan band in the 1930s and with such unrecorded legends as Buddy Petit and Chris Kelly.

15. Adolphe Paul Barbarin, drums (May 5, 1899–February 17, 1969). Left New Orleans in 1918 and played in Chicago and New York with King Oliver, Luis Russell, Louis Armstrong, and Jelly Roll Morton. Composer of such Dixieland standards as "Bourbon Street Parade," "Come Back, Sweet Papa" and "Second Line." Back in New Orleans, he led his own bands from the mid-1950s on.

16. Samuel Barclay Charters, banjo, cornet, piano, writer, documentarian (August 1, 1929–), was active in a number of fields over several decades, but one of his most influential works (the book referred to here) is *Jazz, New Orleans, 1885–1963: An Index to the Negro Musicians of New Orleans*.

17. Joe "Brother Cornbread" Thomas, clarinet (December 3, 1902–February 18, 1981). Recorded with Oscar Celestin in 1951, the Olympia Brass Band in 1963, and Punch Miller in 1961. One of the last of the old-style Creole clarinet players.

18. Emile "Milé" Barnes, clarinet (February 18, 1892–March 2, 1970). Musically active from the dawn of Dixieland music, his professional career was from 1908 to 1966. As a teenager, he hung around with the great Sidney Bechet, whose influence is discernible in his playing—or is it the other way round?

19. Joe Watkins (Mitchell Watson), drums (October 24, 1900–September 13, 1969). Another musician who came to prominence with the George Lewis band during its halcyon years, Watkins was forced to retire from music in 1966 because of arthritis and died in abject poverty.

20. Louis Hall Nelson, trombone (September 17, 1902–April 5, 1990). After playing with Sidney Desvigne and Buddy Petit, Nelson joined the Kid Thomas band in 1944 and stayed for four decades. He was an extremely versatile player and could play smooth legato melodies in the manner of his idol, Tommy Dorsey, or play hot and extrovertedly when the occasion demanded.

21. Wilhelmina "Billie" Pierce (née Goodson), piano (June 8, 1907–September 29, 1974). Sister to Sadie and Ida Goodson, both of whom also played piano. Married De De Pierce in 1935, and the two of them worked at Luthjen's dance hall for more than twenty years. According to Earl Palmer, people would go to their performances just to see them fight!

22. Joseph La Croix "De De" Pierce, trumpet (February 18, 1904–November 23, 1973). De De was an explosive and forceful player from French-speaking stock. Widely credited in New Orleans as the composer of "Eh la Bas," he allegedly won a French-speaking competition against the mayor of Lafayette, Louisiana, by knowing the French word for *monkey wrench*.

23. Andrew Blakeney, trumpet (June 10, 1898–February 12, 1992). Replaced Louis Armstrong in the King Oliver band in Chicago in 1925. Moved to Los Angeles, where he played with Les Hite's orchestra around 1930 and Lionel Hampton became his protégé. From 1935 to 1941, he lived in Hawaii; then he returned to Los Angeles and played with Kid Ory from 1947 to 1949.

24. Joseph Wilmer Darensbourg, clarinet and saxophone (July 9, 1906–May 24, 1985). Worked with Fate Marable on the riverboats around 1920, then briefly with Jelly Roll Morton and Kid Ory in the 1940s and 1950s, and replaced Barney Bigard in the Louis Armstrong All Stars in 1961.

25. "Captain" John Guy Handy, saxophone and clarinet (June 24, 1900–January 12, 1971). One of New Orleans's most exciting musicians, his searing alto sax playing was said to have influenced both Earl Bostic and Louis Jordan.

26. Reprinted from Mick Burns, *The Great Olympia Band* (Jazzology Press, 2001).

27. Andrew "Big" Morgan, clarinet and saxophone (March 19, 1903–September 19, 1972). Took his first lessons from Albert Nicholas and recorded with his brother Sam Morgan's band in 1927. Played around New Orleans with Kid Thomas, Alphonse Picou, Herb Morand, and Peter Bocage. Subsequently took over the leadership of the Young Tuxedo Brass Band.

28. Alton Purnell, piano (April 16, 1911–January 14, 1987). A great two-handed piano player and vocalist of outstanding sincerity and swing. He was recruited into the Bunk Johnson band when it went to New York in 1945 and then worked with George Lewis for the next decade. Purnell moved to Los Angeles in 1956.

29. Albert Nicholas, clarinet (May 27, 1900–September 3, 1973). Left New Orleans to join King Oliver in Chicago in 1924. Toured the Middle East until 1928 and then joined the Luis Russell band, with which he stayed for twelve years. After 1953, he lived most of the time in Europe. Another great New Orleans original.

30. Ben Webster, tenor saxophone (March 27, 1909–September 20, 1973). One of the unique jazz voices that elevated the Duke Ellington band of the early 1940s, he is probably best remembered for his storming solo on the recording "Cottontail"; the solo was later scored by Benny Carter for a full saxophone section, a high accolade indeed. However, Webster was given to irascibility: hearing himself announced by Ellington on stage as being featured on the next number, he threw his saxophone at the orchestra leader's head, shouting, "Here! Play the son of a bitch yourself!"

31. Ray Nance, trumpet and violin (December 10, 1913–January 28, 1976). After a spell with the Earl Hines Orchestra, he replaced Cootie Williams in the Ellington band in 1941, where the other band members included Ben Webster, Barney Bigard, and Lawrence Brown. His solo on the famous recording of "Take the A Train" became mandatory for the trumpet players who followed him (including, much later, Cootie Williams).

32. Hoagland Howard "Hoagy" Carmichael, piano, composer (November 22, 1899–December 27, 1981). Although a more than competent entertainer, his greatest legacy is the wealth of great songs he wrote. Without such compositions as "Stardust," "The Nearness of You," "Skylark," "Memphis in June," and "Baltimore Oriole," the golden era of American popular song wouldn't have been.

33. Quoted in Bill Russell, *New Orleans Style* (Jazzology Press, 1994).

34. Barney Bigard, *With Louis and the Duke: The Autobiography of a Jazz Clarinetist*, edited by Barry Martyn (Macmillan, 1985). Reproduced with permission of Palgrave Macmillan.

35. Lawrence Brown, trombone (August 3, 1907–September 6, 1988). After a total of more than twenty-five years as featured soloist with Duke Ellington, he left the orchestra permanently in 1970, following a fistfight with the leader. On his way to Los Angeles, Brown stopped at his aunt's house, left his trombone behind her rocking chair, and never went back for it.

36. William Randolph "Cozy" Cole, drums (October 17, 1909–January 31, 1981). During his long career, he formed musical associations with some of the most illustrious names in jazz, including Jelly Roll Morton, Billie Holiday, Benny Goodman, Charlie Parker, Stuff Smith, Benny Carter, Cab Calloway, and Louis Armstrong. Despite having a hit single with "Topsy" in the mid-1950s, he still found time to appear in the movie *The Glenn Miller Story*.

37. Benny Carter, saxophone, trumpet, composer and arranger (August 8, 1907–July 12, 2003). One of the most musically elegant of all jazz musicians, his arrangements, particularly for saxophone sections, are instantly recognizable. Almost the only horn player who could record on equal terms with Art Tatum.

38. Joe Venuti, violin (September 16, 1903–August 14, 1978). Played in the Jean Goldkette orchestra along with Frankie Trumbauer and Bix Beiderbecke, and recorded extensively in the 1920s and 1930s. Known for his waggish sense of humor, he regularly sent one-armed trumpet player Wingy Manone a birthday present of a single cufflink.